The Springs of Enchantment

1

The Springs of Enchantment

Climbing and Exploration in Patagonia

JOHN EARLE

HODDER AND STOUGHTON
LONDON SYDNEY AUCKLAND TORONTO

British Library Cataloguing in Publication Data

Earle, John
    The springs of enchantment.
    1. Patagonia – Description and travel
    I. Title
    918.2'7'046   F2936

    ISBN 0 340 24304 X

Printed in Great Britain by Lowe & Brydone Printers Ltd., Thetford, Norfolk for Hodder and Stoughton Limited, Mill Road, Dunton Green, Sevenoaks, Kent.

Hodder and Stoughton Editorial Office: 47 Bedford Square, London WC1B 3DP.

Contents

ACKNOWLEDGEMENT

Sadly, news of Oliver Bridges' death came while this book was in proof. I shall always remember with gratitude the magnificent hospitality at Viamonte and the help he gave unstintingly.
I should like to thank Phyllis Wint for the generous encouragement and help she gave me during the early planning of my 1979 expedition. My grateful thanks are also due to my father, Geoffrey Earle, for checking the early manuscript of the book and for his many practical suggestions; and my editor, Margaret Body, at Hodders for kind but judicious editing. Last but far from least I should like to acknowledge with love the understanding, patience and encouragement of my wife, Pauline, who made the 1979 expedition possible, and my thanks to my two sons, Robin and Crispin, for looking after her while I was away.

J.E.

Illustrations

Acknowledgments

[1] Reproduced from *Uttermost Part of the Earth* by courtesy of David Bridges.

[2] Don Sargeant.

Maps

1

Patagonia bound

The airline company were on the telephone again. "We are sorry, Mr. Earle. The flight to Buenos Aires has been postponed." I looked out of the window at the thick blanket of snow and the whirl of flakes. The house across the road was only just visible. "Why bother to go on an expedition?" I thought rather grimly; "I might as well stay here and sledge across Barnes Common."

The walk upstairs from the telephone reminded me rather forcibly of the farewell party I had been given last night by the friends I was staying with in Barnes, and I was really quite glad I was not off after all.

The next few days worked me into a caged frenzy of frustration. Everything was ready. Or was it? The last frantic shopping trips were over. But I still had minor panics and doubts and had to rush upstairs to check in my rucksack to make sure that I had packed my gloves and string vests.

New Year's Eve came and went. Not in Rio de Janeiro or Buenos Aires, as I had romantically hoped, but in a taxi, in a snow drift, in the Fulham Road. At least Christopher

Wordsworth, Chris Oliver and I had a bottle of Scotch with us to keep up morale.

That party in the taxi had heralded the arrival of 1963, as I was waiting to fly to South America, for an expedition with Eric Shipton to Patagonia and Tierra del Fuego.

Like many young climbers who are also teachers I had moved towards Outward Bound in the early 1950s and gone to work at the Outward Bound School at Eskdale where Eric Shipton had just been appointed Warden.

We live in a world now where "hero" is almost a dirty word; a cynical world of hard men on the mountains who are almost anti-heroes. Yet for me as a boy in the 1930s and 1940s it was different.

Eric Shipton had been my childhood hero. I had read avidly all the mountaineering books I could get hold of and many of them were books that Eric himself had written or in which his travels and climbs were featured. The character of the man began to emerge through the written word and it soon became apparent that he stood for all that I was beginning to yearn for and feel about exploring and mountaineering.

It was therefore a slightly starry-eyed young man who had turned up at the Outward Bound centre in an ancient red MG called Alpine Aggie, with a leg in plaster as a result of a rugger injury. Twenty-five years later this first meeting with Eric Shipton remains in the memory; the shy, retiring approach, the piercing blue eyes, a nose that had been broken in a recent car accident in the narrow Eskdale lanes, the unruly white hair, and bushy eyebrows.

Of course it is known now that Eric had not been happy about his appointment as Warden at Eskdale. He felt, and he was right, of course, that while he loved talking and com-municating with people, he was too much of an introvert to be a highly successful Warden and leader of youth. Many of the boys on the courses had no idea what an outstanding man they had as their Warden. Few took advantage of his ability to talk and discuss things with small groups of individuals; to argue for the pure delight of argument, calling black, white and white, black, if needs be.

What he did do, however, was to inspire his staff to run exciting and imaginative courses that were perhaps amateur in the true sense of the word. Particularly so in comparison with the very professional present-day world of outdoor pursuits, plagued as it is with certificates, diplomas and qualifications; where every activity is analysed for its "carry over" values, its meaning and its effect.

Eric also brought fun and laughter to the Outward Bound. He had a very finely developed sense of humour that did not necessarily show itself by loud laughter, but his sense of the ridiculous was enormous. A ludicrous ballet dance that Roy Greenwood and I did, with our hairy legs fully exposed below frilly ballet skirts amused him tremendously. I also remember with joy Eric standing up with the other instructors at the same end of course Christmas concert where we had performed our ballet, to sing to a well known hymn tune, "We are the outward bounders no earthly use are we. All we want is breakfast, supper, lunch and tea." It ended, "Blow you Jack, I'm all right"!

After this Outward Bound interlude we both went our various ways, but at Eskdale a friendship was born and my early inspiration from reading Eric's books continued through knowing the man himself, as we kept in contact with letters and occasional meetings.

Eric went on to work in forestry, "to restore my serenity" as he puts it, after the breakdown of his marriage, but by 1957, the call of the wild, lonely places caught him again and in 1958 he made the first of six expeditions to the "uttermost part of the earth", Tierra del Fuego and Patagonia. A second phase, one might almost say, in his exploration had started.

It is no wonder that this remote and storm-lashed land should have attracted him. He was always fascinated by early explorers and writers, particularly of this region – Magellan, Drake, Darwin. The tip of South America offered him what he looked for, unexplored regions with all the problems of travel in such remote areas; not necessarily summits to be climbed, but because they were there, obviously a chance to attempt to reach them as well.

Without doubt the most incredible of these expeditions was his fearful 250-mile journey across the Patagonian ice-cap in fifty-two days of unbelievable hardship and work.

Seven hundred and twenty pounds of equipment and food had to be relayed up through the forest and steep, broken ground to the glaciers and ice-cap beyond. It was nine days before the sledge could be used; even then two relays were necessary. Soft snow and lack of sledge-hauling experience made these early days utterly exhausting. Added to this, Eric suffered an accident that could have proved disastrous, when he emptied a full billy-can of boiling water over his naked foot and for a week became a reluctant sledge passenger. After seventeen days they reached the glacial plateau.

Day after day the routine was the same: up at three thirty a.m., breakfast, packing up, digging the ice and snow from around the tent and the buried sledges and harnesses; trying to set off at seven thirty a.m.; sledging all day, for most of the time by compass bearing in thundering gales and blinding drifts; stopping at three p.m., and cooking a meal after getting the tent up, and sleep by seven thirty p.m. After four weeks they were halfway there and reached some ground already explored by Eric, but the pattern was still the same, with savage blizzards, luckily mostly from behind them, and periods of calm. Then, on January 30th, having set out on December 11th, they reached the gentle woodlands and birdsong of the Estancia la Cristina. It was over. A classic Shipton journey.

After leaving Eskdale I also changed my job, from teaching to working for television as an expedition cameraman and freelance broadcaster. In 1961 I went with John Tyson on my first expedition, to the Kanjiroba Himal. The next year Eric invited me to join him on his expedition to South America in early 1963. It was typical of him to help me with my new career. Indeed he helped so many, either directly by taking them on his expeditions, or by his wise counsel to young men planning to explore remote parts of the world. If anyone came to him with the spark of an idea, he always received the same enthusiastic advice – to go and do it.

In September, I had driven up to Wiltshire to see him and to discuss early plans, and then later we met several times in London. Those golden autumnal days always seemed to be fine. Low banks of mist hung over the London parks. The air was crisp and bracing as we walked across to the Royal Geographical Society to pore over maps. I shared with Eric a love of London at this time of year; so many plans and dreams seemed to have evolved on such days.

On several occasions I drove with Eric to keep some appointment. His driving was splendidly erratic and vague. He would talk almost incessantly about expedition plans, or recount one of his intriguing stories, swerving in and out of the traffic lanes, crossing red lights, even once going the wrong way up a one-way street. He knew London streets very well, but often would forget in which direction he was supposed to be going and we would have to stop, think about it, and start again.

One of the jobs we had to do at this time was to vacuum-pack the food. This was a new process that had just recently been developed. We spent quite a bit of time in the East End doing this work, weighing out the sugar and porridge which seemed to form the main part of the rations. We also paid a visit to the huge block of the Horlicks factory at Slough to talk to Adrian de Jong, who was a dietician and an expedition ration expert. He was responsible for developing the first-rate expedition rations which Horlicks produced in the 1950s and '60s, including the excellent meat bars that I personally still yearn for on expeditions. Adrian de Jong was able to provide the number of these bars we needed and one or two other rations for the expedition including, of course, Horlicks malted milk.

The other slightly comic interlude at this time was a visit to Price's Patent Candle Factory in London, where Eric was made to pose for publicity photographs pretending to chew a candle that was reputed to have calorific value and could even supplement our rations! I know he inwardly squirmed with embarrassment at this sort of publicity, but with extreme goodwill he chewed away at his candle for the benefit of the photographers.

On the whole Eric found food a tiresome necessity as a fuel to keep him going, though he did have a weakness for kippers and had them for breakfast every day for quite a number of years. But he discovered cooking with a naïve delight. Not that he had a wide range of dishes and most of his culinary art was a determination to prove that a person could live on one and sixpence (7½p) worth of food a day. Later he agreed that it had crept up to half a crown (12½p). Heaven knows what he would think of today's prices, but he had seen inflation in Hungary and predicted that we would soon be faced with similar problems here.

His favourite dish was vegetable curry and whenever I smell curry cooking, I see again Eric mixing a roux (he was fascinated by this and thrilled to find it easy) and stirring in the curry powder. The sauce was poured over the half-cooked vegetables, often marrow which he loved, and then left to simmer. Served with boiled rice it was indeed a cheap, tasty and quick meal and one I often ate with him at the flat in Tite Street.

As on his expeditions, the other great standby for Eric was porridge. Mainly, I suspect, because Quaker Oats had mis-understood his requirements for one expedition and had donated several large sacks instead of a few packets. One of these sacks stood open in the kitchen for years and at every breakfast large, steaming saucepans of porridge appeared.

The food and the small amount of equipment that Eric had decided to take had been shipped out to Punta Arenas by the Pacific Steam Navigation Company in October. At last, when everything seemed ready for our departure, Eric suddenly stopped as we were walking back to his Kensington flat on the evening before the flight.

"We haven't got the Vitamin C tablets," he said. "I am sure massive overdoses prevent chills and colds."

We strode off again looking for a chemist open at that time of night. It must have been after nine o'clock and we had walked miles before Eric remembered the all-night chemist at Piccadilly Circus. We both looked and felt completely out of place in our tweed jackets, shirts and ties in that Piccadilly chemists at eleven p.m., surrounded by drunks, drug addicts and hypochondriacs, as the bemused assistant served Eric with 2,000 Vitamin C tablets. She must have thought he had become hooked on them. Later on the expedition Eric was to hand out to each of us, without fail, every night, with our supper, our five Vitamin C tablets. Eric was right; none of us caught a cold during the expedition.

On New Year's Day, after our delay by heavy snow, we set out at last for South America. Eric wore his heavy climbing boots to save weight with what already seemed frugal luggage to my eyes, used to Himalayan standards. As we settled down in the plane he turned to me and said, "By the way, have we any tents? I think I may have left one down in Punta Arenas." This marvellous vagueness that I came to understand was not an act. To him there were more important things to think about in planning an expedition than his tent.

ONE

1963

2

Punta Arenas and points west

The Comet rose steeply out of the snow and fog of Heath-
row. Paris was cold and wet, Madrid cloudy and dank, and
then Dakar at three a.m. – we stepped out into the humid,
heavy tropical night full of the sound of crickets and the smell
of sun-baked earth. The heat was solid and my tweed suit
stuck to me with sweat. On again. Brazil – Rio de Janeiro
from the air, the Sugarloaf Mountain, the Statue of Christ.
Then, almost before I was aware of it, we were having a pre-
breakfast swim in a pool belonging to friends of Eric with
whom we were staying in Buenos Aires. London with its fog
and snow seemed ages away.

The DC3 that rumbled its way on towards the south
seemed, after the speed of the Comet, to be hovering, but we
flew on, now over arid, brown, rolling grasslands with
occasional tracks snailing to remote farms. Minute blobs pin-
pointed the treeless plains. This was cattle and sheep country.
For the last hour we moved over a strange moonscape, a red
plateau dotted with volcanic cones. Then, without warning,
we were coming down over the deep blue Magellan Straits,

with wind-whipped white waves surging towards the Atlantic, to land at the airport of Punta Arenas, which was at this time considered the southernmost city in the world. Today there is an Argentinian challenge from Ushuaia.

It was a chill, windy day, even though it was supposed to be summer, as we clambered into the ramshackle bus that was waiting to take us the fifteen miles to the city. At last we were off along the stony track from the airport. A cloud of brown, swirling dust rose chokingly behind us and into the bus itself, through the many cracks and holes. The wireless blared out advertising jingles as we rattled and swayed around the corners. I looked at my travelling companions. Many were a mixture of Chilean and Indian. Most of them appeared to be either shepherds or workers from the huge refrigeration plants in this region. Indeed, we passed a mob of sheep on the road, 3,000 of them at least, and five shepherds on horseback, sitting squarely on their woollen saddles, protected from the cold wind by their ponchos. At a "freezer" more workers got in and one of them threw half a sheep's carcass on the rack. You never buy less than half a sheep down here apparently. The bus was now packed to the ceiling and the fug was thick with the smell of cheap cigarettes and strong mutton fat soap. The wireless roared. They all shouted and laughed as we banged along the track. Suddenly we were disgorged at Punta Arenas.

The focal point of the city is really the square, Munoz Gamero, in the middle of which stands the statue of Magellan, pointing south towards the strait named after him, just a quarter of a mile away and visible down the straight streets running down to the water's edge. Round the stone pedestal, on which the statue stands, are Indians representing the tribes Magellan must have seen and whose fires prompted him to call the island to the south of the strait, Tierra del Fuego, Land of Fire. The foot of one of the Indians juts out and can be easily reached from the ground. The toes are shining and brightly polished, for a strange legend has it that if you kiss, or even touch the foot, it will bring you luck and you will return again and again to Puntas Arenas. A surprising number of passers-by do touch the Indian's foot and the countless hands keep the bronze gleaming.

It is a city of extraordinary contrasts. Attempts were made to settle on the Magellan Straits by the Spaniard Sarmiento in 1584, partly as a reaction to Drake's voyages and discoveries in this part of the world, and partly because of his raid on Callao. This pitiful attempt to colonise the area was a disastrous affair; a story of acute human suffering, hardship and tragedy. So it was not until 1843 that the city was founded. A few old houses survive and much of Punta Arenas has the look and feeling of a North European city rather than a Spanish colonial town as in the rest of South America. The reason for this is that it was the Spaniards, Yugoslavs, British, French and Germans who settled and lived here in those early days and who, indeed, still live and trade here. The buildings and the faces are European.

In 1963 some 40,000 people lived in Punta Arenas and while the centre of the city looked clean, modern and prosperous, with shops selling the consumer goods of our times, you did not have to walk far to find the suburbs of corrugated iron, or metal sheets. Even near the centre, many of the older houses were made of wood and corrugated iron and yet the proportions were good, with the beautifully made wooden doors and windows one would expect to see on a Georgian brick house in Britain.

Paved and surfaced roads were found only in the city itself and even there many of the back streets were just dirt tracks full of pot-holes with grass growing through the cracked pavements. Like many modern American cities, Punta Arenas was planned in blocks with straight inter-connecting streets, and as many of these streets, even in the shanty areas, are broad and many of the houses single-storeyed, there is a great feeling of space and sky. The only snag is that, because of these straight streets, strong summer storms shriek up from the Pacific and the wind makes walking almost imposs-ible.

Eric and I were staying at the guest house of the slaughter-house and refrigeration plant in a small village called Rio

Seco, about five miles outside Punta Arenas. It was a long, wooden building with little rooms leading off a long corridor, where people stayed when they came to buy wool, meat and skins from the company who ran the "freezer". A man called Cyril Jarvis lived in the guest house all the time. He was the engineer of the plant and needed to be on call twenty-four hours a day during the season. Cyril, as well as being an engineer was also a radio ham and his little room was crowded to the ceiling with wirelesses and electrical gear of all sorts. I woke up several times in the early hours of the morning, to hear him calling away to some other ham on the other side of the world, the wooden building full of the sound of static, crackling and fizzing from the ionosphere, and the Donald Duck quacking of some distant operator.

To look after us and give us our meals, Mrs Nancy Stewart had stayed on as housekeeper, though in fact very few business guests now came to stay. She was a short, bustling, grey-haired lady with perceptive eyes behind glasses. Nancy was used, it would seem, to dealing with untidy, vague males who came and went, leaving behind piles of dirty laundry and empty plates after her gargantuan meals. Kindly and efficient, she got us ready for the expedition and indeed we used the garage of her house in Punta Arenas as a store for all our gear and equipment that had by now arrived by sea from Britain.

Her brother, Alex Booth, who lived with her, was immensely stout and he also was a radio ham. The corner of their living room was yet another radio station and he would put through calls not only to Cyril Jarvis five miles away up the road at Rio Seco, but to the Falkland Islands, where relatives lived. All over South America, Tierra del Fuego and the Falklands, remote estancia owners use radios to keep in touch and relay vital messages.

Alex was invaluable to us during the waiting period in Punta Arenas. He knew everyone and everything and he made many of the contacts and appointments we needed, before we were ready to set off.

A CIRCUMNAVIGATION OF MOUNT BURNEY

STRAITS OF MAGELLAN

Punta Arenas

FitzRoy Channel

Rio Verde

Estancia Skyring

SENO SKYRING

Beagle Bay

SENO OTWAY

Punta Laura

PENINSULA

ISLA RIESCO

Obstruction Sound

Passo del Indio

MT INACCESSIBLE

MT TRYFAN 2
TRYFAN 1

MT BURNEY

MUNOZ GAMERO PENINSULA

Isla Lota

Mayne Channel

SMYTH CHANNEL

STRAITS OF MAGELLAN

PACIFIC OCEAN

Miles
Km

Cape Horn

Miles
Km

23

Our first objective was a mysterious volcanic peak called Mount Burney on the Munoz Gamero peninsula in south-west Chilean Patagonia, 140 miles north-west of Punta Arenas. It had often been referred to as the most southerly active volcano in South America and Eric had always been fascinated by volcanoes. There was a vague report that in 1910 it had been seen erupting, and andecite lava had been collected on its west side, near the Mayne Channel. As far as could be seen, Mount Burney was a peak guarded by thick forests, unknown lakes, mountains and weather completely unpredictable and violent. No one had succeeded in getting near it, but in 1962, after one of his other trips with a Chilean friend called Cedomir Marangunic, Eric had got within twelve miles, by hitherto unexplored and unknown lakes not even marked on the very poor maps of the area. Lack of time and the difficulties of the country had made it impossible for them to get any closer, so Eric had decided to devote some time to investigating the area further now. He had invited Jack Ewer, who had been with him on several of his early expeditions, including the ice-cap crossing, to join us for this journey. Jack now lived in Chile and lectured in English at Santiago University.

It soon became apparent that Eric was a welcome visitor to this part of Chile. The various officials whom we met were friendly and helpful, including a general from the Chilean army, who made the arrangements for a lorry with a driver to be put at our disposal for the first part of our expedition.

On January 8th, when we arrived back at Mrs. Stewart's house after lunch at the guest house at Rio Seco, the lorry was waiting to be loaded. Alex Booth, Eric, Jack and I carried out from the garage the food and equipment we needed for a month. There was also the massive bundle of the RFD inflatable boat, as well as the ten horse-power Evinrude outboard engine, with forty gallons of petrol. All this nearly filled the back of the small army lorry, so poor Jack Ewer, who had elected to travel there for the first part of the journey, had to be levered into place on top of the load. He was a tall, gangling, wiry man with a splendid cynical sense

24

of humour and a marvellous assortment of slightly eccentric expedition clothing either made by himself or his wife, including a voluminous shirt, with tails that almost reached his ankles, and baggy Elizabethan sleeves. He was a man of firm, unwavering beliefs and, like Eric, enjoyed argument. It seemed as if my role during the expedition was going to be that of referee.

One of my other jobs was to make a film for the BBC's Adventure series and Traveller's Tales. As the lorry jerked and jolted its way out of Punta Arenas, for the young army driver did not seem very competent, I filmed our progress past the delightful statue of a shepherd with his horse, dog and sheep which stands at the outskirts of the city. After that, I squeezed into the cab with Eric and the driver, while muffled shouts from Jack, demanding to know why we were going so slowly, floated out from the back of the lorry.

We were soon off the metalled road, and ahead stretched a dusty track across the flat, arid plain. Every few miles we were juddered by long sections of corrugated road, with small undulations about two feet apart, caused by bouncing vehicles. The secret is to drive pretty fast and so keep on top of the bumps; the young army driver had not discovered this trick.

By late afternoon we had reached the head of Seno Otway and were following a road along the incredibly narrow strait that runs from Beagle Bay into the Fitzroy Channel: historic names and historic places, for this channel, discovered by Fitzroy, runs into Seno Skyring and links these two great inland waters.

At Rio Verde on Seno Skyring we let the poor dusty Jack out of the back, looking like a miller at the end of his day's work. We were given some petrol at a saw mill, and I clambered into the back for the journey to Estancia Skyring where we arrived at about seven fifteen.

This was the first estancia I had seen and I was astonished by the feeling of luxury, for this was a remote and lonely place on the shores of the Sound, with forest and rolling hills close by and in the distance snow-covered peaks. The garden outside was a blaze of colour with flowers of all kinds. The house itself was made of wood and corrugated iron, but the proportions of the rooms and windows made it most attractive. The rooms were large, comfortable and well furnished, while in one of them was a full-size billiard table. Beyond the house were several out-buildings and small cottages where the workers lived, also made of wood with red-painted corrugated iron roofs. The largest building of all was the huge shearing shed, like an enormous hangar, with pens full of pink, naked-looking, new-shorn sheep outside. It seemed a prosperous and contented place and after a good meal with our host Gerald Friedli, we all slept well in comfortable beds.

We were brought a cup of tea in bed at about six forty-five – our last little bit of soft living – and after an early breakfast we set off once again in the lorry along a rough, muddy track that wound through the forest of nothofagus trees (the Southern beech) many of which had been burnt to clear the land for more grazing. Great areas of burnt stumps gave the feeling of a battlefield after armies had passed through. Many of the dead and burnt trees had fallen across the track and we had to heave and haul them out of the way. Soon we were into parts of the endless forest that had never been cleared or thinned since the beginning of time. Weird curtains of straggling green lichen festooned the grey branches and many fallen trees, covered in moss, were gradually rotting back into the landscape.

The young Chilean army driver had obviously never driven in country like this before. We crawled along, stopping and starting, jerking and jolting. Suddenly, Eric could stand it no longer and suggested that he should take over. We moved faster after that. It was a very different Eric from the one that I had driven with in London; forceful and skilful. Many times the track disappeared and Eric took the lorry over smooth grass along the edge of Seno Skyring and even on the beach itself. The water was a deep blue and black-necked swans paddled offshore, hardly noticing our rumbling progress.

26

Several sections of the track had narrow, rickety bridges that sagged as Eric drove the lorry over them in four-wheel drive. When we reached areas of marsh, lines of small logs had been laid across the surface to form what is called "corduroy" track, and they kept the lorry from sinking in. However, on a long section of a hundred yards or more the logs had rotted and, as the lorry tried to clamber out on the far side up the hill, the wheels started to spin and soon we were in almost up to the axles. Luckily there was a winch on the front and by attaching a wire to a tree, Eric was able to haul the lorry out by its own power. Halfway up the hill the engine failed and all was an awful silence. Even if he was not much of a driver, the army corporal did know about the mechanics of his lorry, and within minutes he had the petrol pump in bits, cleaned and put together again. This time all was well and we ground on to our destination, a small bay. Beyond, the forest was trackless and clearly the lorry could go no further.

We unloaded all the gear and carried it for half a mile, in relays, along the beach and over a small peninsula to a bay on the other side. The lorry started back with the young corporal once again crouching nervously at the wheel and on his own. I think we all wondered if he would make it safely back to the estancia some fifteen miles away.

We now began the job of blowing up the large RFD inflatable dinghy by means of two foot-pumps, a job we were to repeat many times in the next few weeks. It took about twenty minutes and we developed a comic one-legged dance, bouncing up and down on the pumps. Next, all the food and equipment and the eight jerry-cans of petrol were packed in the bows, which left just enough room for us to sit at the stern, and we were all set to go. The outboard engine failed to start and we tinkered about with it on the shore until, for no apparent reason, it roared into life and we set off.

By this time a strong wind had blown up, whipping spray back over the bows of the RFD. Within minutes we were soaked to the skin. But the sky was still blue and the water sparkling, even if it was cold. As if to welcome us, dolphins began to surf in the bow wave, tumbling over and over, turning their white bellies up to the sky, escorting us on our way.

We had been told by Gerald Friedli to look out for two small wooden huts on a low cliff and, sure enough, just before dusk we sighted them and two peons nearby waving us in. The huts, used by shepherds during round-ups, were like the pre-war Alpine huts. In the warmth round the fire we dried our wet clothes and had a good meal. The wind howled outside, whipping the Sound into long streamers of foam and shaking the wooden walls, but we slept soundly on our air-mattresses by the wood stove.

The two shepherds left at dawn, and after breakfast we packed our gear into the boat and cruised across the bay to where they had lit a fire to guide us in to the landing beach. We took everything out of the boat, let out the air, rolled it up and put it into its valise. The two peons started to tie all the kit bags, boxes and petrol cans on to the backs of four pack-horses. They had not enough rope, so one of our climbing ropes had to be unpacked and used to lash every-thing on. I strapped the outboard engine on to a pack frame and hoisted it on to my back. It weighed about seventy-five pounds. At last we were ready for the first relay up the steep hill and over an isthmus to the other side. The reason for this manoeuvre was to avoid rounding Punta Laura at the end of the Diadena peninsula, where forcing westward in a small boat against the wind might have been a hazardous opera-tion.

The horses took an instant dislike to us and tried to scrape their heavy loads off on to the trees as they zig-zagged up the hill. One succeeded in knocking the whole load round until it was hanging underneath its belly, while another drove a sharp branch through one of the plastic petrol-cans and covered itself and the rest of the load in petrol. The two peons shouted and tugged at their horses. Eric, Jack and I, all with heavy loads on our backs, tried to control the mounting excitement and terror of the horses, and for one moment it looked as though the whole operation was going to end in disaster then and there. It made a good sequence for the film I was shooting, but the best shots of all would have been of myself.

As I had to stop to re-tie the load on the back of my horse, I was left behind and then lost my way in the forest and swamp, when we approached the other side. While I staggered on with the ten horse-power Evinrude motor on my back, the horse I was leading sank fairly deeply into the bog and in an effort to get out, fell over on top of me. I was squashed into the marsh by the weight of the horse and the motor and had an unbelievable struggle trying to get myself and the animal to our feet. I arrived at the shore soaked, flattened, covered in mud, with a frayed temper, and not very kindly feelings for the wretched animal. Jack wanted to know what had kept me! I told him – through clenched teeth!

Eric, who had always been a good horseman, revelled in this interlude and while he rode back with the peons and the horses to bring the second relay over, Jack and I sorted out the gear and started to pump up the boat again, dancing on the pumps until the muscles in our legs ached.

There was a tremendous wind blowing, lashing the brown waters of the fiord into large waves that pounded on to the west-facing beach. Obviously, we were not going to be able to launch the boat here and we had to move everything across into the lee of an island. When Eric arrived with the loads and I had filmed the peons setting out back to the estancia, with a look of stunned bewilderment on their faces at the thought of our being left at the edge of the unknown, we made a huge fire and brewed up, while we waited for the wind to drop.

In what appeared to be a lull we launched into the waves and just got off without being swamped. The rollers on the main lake were huge and we plunged up and down, slowly westward. Again within minutes we were soaked and we constantly had to bail out the boat as the water swirled around our feet. On one edge of the Sound the waves lessened, and as it was nearly dark we found a little beach and pitched the tents there. Behind rose a black and impenetrable wall of forest. It was the only place for our tents, and Eric assured us that the tides were extremely small in these inland seas.

We cooked our meal on a wood fire and listened to the wind roaring in the trees above us and across the water a few hundred yards away. I felt very tired. It suddenly struck me that this really was the start of it all. It had been happening gradually. A slow withdrawal from civilisation, bit by bit. With the return of the peons to the estancia and our launching out on to the rough Sound we had severed the final link. We were truly on our way.

3

A tour of the lakes

I woke at five a.m. to the sound of lapping water, and on looking out of the door of the tent I saw that the tide had risen to within a foot of the entrance. Luckily we were on a sheltered shore and, as Eric had said, the tides were small here; I went to sleep again until nine o'clock. This time I woke to the sound of Jack brewing a cup of tea and cooking breakfast. The tide was still high, with only about ten feet between the water and the forest.

Eric had a chill from the soaking of the previous day and stayed in bed while Jack bailed out the boat and tried to rig a large polythene sheet as a spray deck. I clambered up into the thick forest and found the going really very difficult. It would have been impossible to travel easily on land. It was an extraordinary, dank, lush area of vegetation, with ferns and mosses growing on the tree trunks. Like all thick forests it was very silent, except for eight little wrens that had been following me about. They chirruped and scolded with rage as I crouched on the forest's ferny floor, obeying a sudden call of nature. Quite right too! It must have been a startling sight. Back at the camp, Eric was up and busily drying his socks and boots around the fire, as we had our lunch. Then, as the wind dropped, we packed everything up and loaded it once again into the boat. It did not take us long this time as we were beginning to drop into a routine.

We launched and were off through the narrow channels. Once again the wind was fierce but it eased as we struck out, after six miles, into the wider part of the fiord. As we dodged in and out of the islands we tried the fishing rod over the stern. All went well, until Eric, shifting position to get out of the spray, knocked the rod overboard. It sank in a moment and so ended our hopes of fish to stretch our meagre rations.

As we reached the main fiord, the waves became frighteningly large; great rollers towering over the small rubber boat. We felt glad we had our life-jackets, but how long we would have survived in the icy waters, if we had gone overboard, is doubtful. The wind increased, and once again we were soaked through. Water swilled around on the floor and bailing was a constant job for one of us all the time.

We had just rounded the point of a peninsula when the painter, which had fallen unnoticed into the water, fouled the propeller and we started to drift helplessly towards the rocks in the strong winds. Being nearest the stern, I plunged my arm in up to the shoulder, trying to free the propeller under the water. Miraculously the rope came loose and, even more miraculously, the engine started and we pulled away to safety just in time.

Fuel was running low and, as filling the tank at sea was a tricky operation, it was with enormous relief that we chugged into the calm of the little bay of Passo del Indio.

This idyllic spot, with wild fuchsias growing at the water's edge, was situated on a narrow isthmus that separates the north-west corner of Sero Skyring from the system of fresh water lakes of the Munoz Gamero peninsula. Although its position had been plotted from aerial photographs, no one had visited the area until Eric came this way the year before us, and there was no firm evidence that this was the precise place where the Alacaluf Indians had had to portage their

canoes over from Obstruction Sound to the southern channels. But, even allowing for wishful thinking, it did seem
pretty likely that we had found the Passo del Indio.

The film I was making for television occupied a lot of my
thoughts. I constantly had to keep a shooting schedule in my
head, trying to link sequences together and the whole into
one coherent story, with, of course, the future and the ending
completely unknown and unpredictable. The next day we
packed up camp and started to carry the loads over to the
freshwater lake on the other side. I busily filmed the journey
as well as carrying a load myself.

We had a climb of a hundred feet in several short sections.
It was beautiful country, very like Scotland or Wales, but
with more trees. We passed several little lakes. The whole
area was very boggy and we squelched along with heavy
loads and then steeply down for the last hundred yards
through forests to the beach on the far side. After a short rest,
we set off back to the camp with empty pack-frames, and on
our arrival gulped huge draughts of lemonade.

Eric had always maintained that carrying loads was the
only way to get fit for carrying loads. This philosophy gave
rise to the hilarious story of a game-keeper's astonished
reaction on finding Eric carrying sacks of pigmeal up and
down Clee Hill in Shropshire before one of his trips.

For the next journey we took the boat, which, even with
the wooden floorboards removed, still weighed 150 pounds.
It was an appallingly awkward and bulky load and we carried
it for ten-minute spells. Getting to one's feet with it lashed to
the pack-frame on one's back was a terrible struggle, and
once up, it nearly drove us into the ground. One television
critic, after watching this part of my film, referred to Eric as
"this aging masochist" and I must say that the three of us
looked pretty ancient as we tottered on with the huge silver
bundle on our backs. Indeed, there was a strange primitive
thrill of sheer physical effort in getting the load to the other
side.

It was lunchtime when we had finally got the boat to the
freshwater lake. Two more relays to do – a total of six hours

of carrying – and it was finished. As we took the last load down, two condors wheeled round overhead. Perhaps they were waiting for us to drop dead! A hole in the boat had to be mended. The wooden keel had to be lashed together as a bolt had broken, and we were ready once again for the pump dance.

By five o'clock we were off on calm water. For once there was no wind. We did eight miles in under two hours and were looking for a camp-site when the engine failed and refused to start again. Luckily there was a small, west-facing beach looking towards snow-covered mountains, so we rowed in there for the night.

On the shore I cleaned the plug of the engine after a frantic search for the spare parts and spanners, with a mounting fear that they had been left behind or lost. It was a delightful part of the network of channels that we were in, with innumerable inlets, forested shores and great sweeping mountains beyond. It looked gentle and friendly, if lonely. Nobody lived here and no one had been here since the Alacaluf paddled their canoes this way many years ago. But for all its beauty it was a harsh and dangerous country. It would have been incredibly difficult to travel without the boat. My panic about the spares and spanners was justified.

The other thing that worried me in a minor way was the countless red, itchy bumps that had come up over my legs, arms and face. It was real expedition hypochondria that gets out of all proportion when one is tired. I had been bitten by little flies, very similar to those that had plagued me in Nepal eighteen months ago. They seemed to be able to bite right through my socks and shirt. Resentfully I noticed that Eric had been bitten too, but that the only signs he had were small red marks. After a good curry for supper I crept into my sleeping bag to itch and scratch for most of the night. Sleep was not made any easier by the storm that lashed out at us on our exposed beach.

When I awoke, firmly believing that I had not slept at all, we found that the boat had been flooded by the storm. We had not hauled it far enough up the beach. Water had soaked into many of the packages including, as I found to my horror, the film stock. I had that hollow, impotent feeling as I cursed and swore at the rain and at our stupidity in leaving the boat badly beached and unprotected. Had my television film been ruined and my means of making a living been made impossible? Everything needed sorting out and re-packing, including much of the food.

Once again the wind rose and violent storms swept straight at us, and I retreated to my tent to dry my camera gear and recorder. One of the film cameras had jammed and the mini tape recorder was soaked, which made one of the batteries very hot. After changing it I played a test roll. It was one I had recorded in London before I left, of the two children of the people I had been staying with, Debbie and Andrew singing 'In Dulce Jubilo'. A great surge of homesickness and nostalgia caught me by the throat. Here I was, lying in a soaking tent in a raging storm on the shores of an unexplored and unknown lake, listening to children's voices singing Christmas carols. How far away and unreal London seemed! Life for us now had become, as it always does on expeditions, a basic skill of minute-to-minute survival and living; simple, uncomplicated, immediate.

The rain had stopped, so we packed up the wet tents and gear and tried to put to sea, but the engine would not start and in any case the wind kept pounding us back on to the beach. We gave up the struggle and wasted time reading, wandering up the cliff behind the beach, eating lunch and cursing our forced choice of camp-site. The wind still blew. I fiddled with the outboard engine and we made a sort of test tank to hold water, out of the boat cover and tried it. To our surprise and relief it started. We read again in the shelter of a rock. The whole day passed and it looked as if we would have to spend another night here. But as we were cooking our supper, the wind suddenly dropped a little. We rushed about like mad things, getting the boat loaded and gulping hot stew at the same time.

At last we were ready to push off. The engine started and, heading into the cold wind, we got through the narrows towards the snow peaks and glaciers that loomed out of the scudding clouds. Once again the wind increased and the lake became very rough, but we had managed to balance the load better now and the dinghy took the waves more easily.

In the dusk, we sighted a sheltered sandy beach and made for it. It had its back to the wind and was another glorious place. We were not going to make the same mistake again by landing on a windward beach. We soon had a fire going and the tent pitched. It had been a strange day of extraordinarily mixed emotions, which are common when people are on expeditions but not usually experienced all on one day; anger, frustration, boredom, discomfort, nostalgia, homesickness, fear, humour; then, the last and most important of all: contentment and peace. As we sat by the fire and sipped our hot drinks, we looked up to see the Southern Cross in the black night. All seemed well at last.

The next day was to be our last day of travelling across large fiords and lakes. We made good time and reached the end of the big lake by mid-morning, but fouled the propeller trying to get in. Eric remembered the position of his old camp-site of the year before, deep in the forests and sheltered, and soon we were settled in with a fire going to keep us warm in the pouring rain. Eric always felt that getting a fire going and a brew ready was of paramount importance, even before setting up the tent. There is nothing like a fire and a cup of tea for boosting morale.

The poor map of the area showed that this was the end of the lake system, but Eric had a hunch that there might be more lakes further north-west, towards Mount Burney. If there were, it would be an amazing stroke of luck for us, for it would mean we could use the boat to carry the food and equipment, rather than relaying loads through the forests on our backs.

It was therefore with eager anticipation that we set off on a reconnaissance up a shallow valley, in the middle of which was a rocky spur. After sections of swamp and forest, we climbed on to the ridge and made good progress. Forty minutes later we saw a sandy bay ahead. We rushed to the water's edge and stood beside a lake stretching away to the glaciers beyond. It was tremendously exciting and the route to the lake was comparatively easy, as the crest of the rocky spur was free of swamp and forest. Eric was never a person for hanging about, so we returned to the camp, had our cheese and biscuits, and took the first loads to the hidden lake.

Later, by torchlight, I wrote up my diary. "It's good to be here. I hope the route to Mount Burney is easy. It's fine to be amongst snow peaks. A strange country this; dank, dripping forests; constant rain; chill. It looks easy and friendly from a distance, but it is cold and inhospitable when you get into it. Hands and feet have been like a washer woman's all day."

The following day we had to continue relaying the loads, including, of course, the 150 pound boat. We moved together for this, two carrying lighter loads, the third carrying the boat, which he took for a fifteen-minute spell and then swopped over. It took us forty-five minutes to reach the lake this way. I was filming for a lot of the journey and came back by myself, looking for flowers and bright colours to shoot in the otherwise dull green, brown and grey landscape.

Back in the camp to collect the last loads, we left a dump of petrol, as we had also done at the Passo del Indio. But first we had to dismantle the traps we had set for springtails, the common name for Collembola. The word traps suggests some fierce predator, but Collembola are, in fact, microscopic creatures responsible for the decomposition of leaf mould and soil. Eric was collecting them for the British Museum and the method was to fill a plastic funnel with leaf mould and hang it near a fire to dry. Below the spout of the funnel was a little bottle of alcohol. As the leaf mould dried, the Collembola fell down the spout into the alcohol to die, presumably, a marvellous death! Eric had collected them all over the world and indeed had found, near the Beagle Channel, an unknown species which was named after him.

We set off at a fast pace with the last load and arrived at the lake in thirty-two minutes. We soon had the boat inflated and

packed and were on our way, chugging west up the unexplored water. The suspense was gripping. After three miles it
looked as if the lake ended, but with mounting excitement
and relief we found, as we got close to the shore, that, in fact,
it turned at right angles and continued north for another four
miles. We followed it right to the end, where the lake once
again turned at right angles to run almost east through some
narrows.

We landed on a sandy shore, and ahead we could see a huge
plain stretching towards the clouds which we knew must
hide Mount Burney. It was a clear night as we sat around the
fire drying our clothes. We had made it. We were now at
grips with our mountain.

I suppose all expeditions are full of moments of elation
followed by utter despair. My diary says quite bluntly:
"Bloody forest and swamp. What a day. I thought our lovely
sandy camp-site at the head of the lake was too good to be
true."

After breakfast we climbed up through steep forests above
the camp. Soon we emerged from the thickly-crowded trees,
covered in moss and lichen, on to a rocky knoll. We still
could not see Mount Burney, so climbed higher, only to
discover that thick clouds had surged down over the mountains, but it was obvious where the peak was; much further
away than we had hoped. To the north and east we had
magnificent views of dolomite-looking peaks. They were
not the Towers of Paine, but it made us think of Chris
Bonington who we knew was climbing there with a British
expedition. To the south, beyond the unknown lake we had
travelled along, we could see a huge ice-cap and below us
stretched the great plain, which Eric thought might be made
of deposits of volcanic ash.

With my lack of expedition experience, especially in this
part of the world, I felt that the best plan would be to try to
travel along the level we were at, towards Mount Burney.
But both Eric and Jack were agreed that an approach along
the swampy plain would be better. With a television film in
mind, I needed the climax of climbing a peak, but Eric, quite

rightly was keen to explore as much of the area as we could.

Feeling very tired and depressed, I followed the others back down through the forest to pack up the camp, load the boat and set out once more on the lake towards a creek we had seen, from which we thought we could reach the plain. We motored through a great mass of Loggerhead or Steamer duck. These birds cannot fly and when they want to move faster, as they obviously did with us bearing down on them, they flail the water with their wings and skim along the surface, like minute model paddle steamers. They made a good sequence for the film and I cheered up a bit.

We were right; the creek did lead to the plain, so we hauled the boat up and pushed through awkward forest and stunted bushes to a fairly solid dry mound on the edge of the swamp.

Once again Eric showed that gentle, yet forceful urge to keep moving. Within an hour we were setting off up the plain with our first load.

Partly because of the 3,000 feet of film I had with me and the two film cameras, but also because we needed to have eighteen days' supply of food with us, we now had to relay our loads.

It was, as we expected, extremely swampy on the plain; very like the worst parts of Dartmoor, where I live now. It was not long before we had all sunk in up to our knees and our boots, socks and trousers were soaked. Huge areas, again like Dartmoor, quivered and rocked as we squelched over them. It was terribly tiring with our huge seventy-pound loads, and when one gets tired, everything seems to get out of proportion. My depression returned and I inwardly cursed the swamp, the route Eric and Jack had chosen, my load, my film-making. I still felt, quite mistakenly, that we would have been better off in the forests. We dumped our loads and left them out for the night and, feeling very weak, I tottered back after the others to the camp. That night I wrote: "To think we have to carry right up to the end of this bloody place and then fight out through thick, dark forest."

So far we had only had short spells of load-carrying but this day was to be the first of constant relaying for nine hours without a break. We must have been carrying over seventy pounds. What a relief it was to slip out of the awkward pack-frames at the dumping point. Without the crushing load it felt almost as if one would topple over backwards or go floating into the air like moon walkers.

After a while, on a carry like this, one retreats inside oneself. The pain from the shoulder-straps cutting into one's muscles, the aching legs and back all seem to fade, as one adjusts one's breathing to the steady pounding rhythm of walking. Sections of really boggy ground, where one stumbles and nearly falls, break into the rhythm, and one curses and swears, then it's back into daydreams of all sorts. Long-forgotten incidents of the past flood back and crowd away the present.

We had seen, far up the plain on the left, a small, sharp peak at the end of a ridge that obviously led up to Mount Burney which was still hidden in the clouds. It looked for all the world like Tryfan in North Wales and we were determined to get level with this peak by the end of that first day. The last carry did it and we put up our tents by a glacial stream which flowed by the ridge and our "Tryfan", both of which ran at right angles to the plain towards Mount Burney.

Eric and Jack pitched their tent in a dell by a stream, but there was no room for mine as well, so I was up on a bank above them, in the full blast of the wind. Away up the valley, just below the low clouds, we could see glaciers and more rock ridges, but had no clear sight of Mount Burney.

Eric had now decided to follow the northern valley, but it was clear that we were going to have difficulty with the river, which was very fast and obviously glacial, milky-white with moraine. We took our first loads up along the river and dumped them, while Jack found a track by the river and some droppings. We guessed that they must have been made by a guanaco, an animal related to the llama, which inhabits this area.

Having fetched a second load from the camp-site, we set off up this track until we reached a confluence and discovered a tree that had fallen across the river, which we could use as a bridge. It was appallingly slippery and with our huge loads and the raging, milky water lapping only a few inches below our feet, it was a nerve-racking crossing, which we had to teeter over five times in all with our loads. This sequence in my film turned out to be as tense as it really felt, as Eric edged his way over the slippery footholds.

We kept to the right-hand branch of the river and suddenly broke out of the forest into an area of huge boulders but with firm, solid ground to walk on rather than swamp and forest. What a relief it was, and with great excitement we came at last to verdant, alpine meadows with many wild flowers. In the mist we saw the snout of a glacier, a towering mass of rubble and rock, nosing towards the grassy slopes. A storm was raging as we settled into camp, but it was such a marvellous place, in a basin formed by the east face of Mount Burney and a low range of wooded foothills, that we did not mind. It was extremely exhilarating to be right in amongst the mountains and glaciers at last.

4

Mount Burney

We now had a problem to settle and a decision to make. The problem was one that often faces one in the Alps, during a bad season. Were we going to wait for a chance to climb Mount Burney or were we going to keep moving and explore a larger area of this unknown mountain? As yet we had not seen the summit but it looked as if the south-east ridge might prove a possible way to the top. If we wished to climb the mountain and do nothing else, then we needed to establish a camp as high as we could on this ridge, below the clouds, and sit it out waiting for clear weather.

Eric had no difficulty in making the decision. He was not one for peak bagging. Travelling and exploring in unknown mountain ranges had always been his main driving force. He suggested that if we made a journey right round the mountain we should explore a great deal of the country and possibly find out if there had been any recent volcanic activity. It would give a purpose to the expedition and, if by any chance the weather cleared, we still might be in a position to get to the summit.

Jack was fairly disgruntled with this plan. It lacked the same large-scale ambition as the ice-cap crossing he had made with Eric the year before. I was still worried about a climax for the television film, but I think, by now, I had realised that sitting in a tent waiting for the weather to clear would not make a climax either, and from the point of view of morale it would have been disastrous. However tired and wet one gets and ready to give anything for some rest and comfort, as soon as one has days of inactivity one longs to be on the move again. It is one of the strange contradictions of expeditions.

We needed to spy out the lie of the land, so the following morning we set off across the meadows towards the start of the glacier, an area of large erratic blocks and moraine. Eventually we climbed on to the glacier itself which was awkward going, as the ice was covered with stones and grit and it made an extremely slippery, unpredictable route. We could see beside the glacier another small rocky peak which we called Tryfan Two. We climbed a gully and then on to the main ridge, which was all very loose rock. However, we reached the summit easily, at a height of about 1,600 feet.

It had been raining on and off all the time, but now it really lashed out at us and the wind increased. From the top we obtained the views we needed to plan the next moves. Below us were huge glaciers running up into the clouds, to where we knew Mount Burney must be hidden. Away to the north and west we could see the fiords and channels of this highly complicated and indented coastline, including the Smyth Channel. To the east we could see the plain we had trudged up, relaying the loads.

We were soon chilled by the wind and rain and with the clouds beginning to descend even lower, we skidded quickly back down to the camp. Eric moved very well on the treacherous, loose rock and shale. He always seemed in balance and used such little effort in comparison with our sliding and clawing progress. Eventually we followed a long, red moraine ridge down and arrived back at the camp with water running down our necks, up our sleeves and into our boots. We quenched our thirst with a foul brew of tea sweetened with wet sticky sweets.

The day I have just described is typical of many when one is on an expedition. Nothing exciting had happened. We had got very wet and tired. We had some outstanding glimpses of this strange country and we had found the route to follow next day, but nothing else.

When we set out with our loads the following day, I led across the glaciers below Tryfan Two, partly through the maze of open crevasses and partly on wet, soggy snow fields, and eventually clambered up the moraine on the far side. It had taken us nearly four hours to reach a suitable spot, so we hid the loads under some rocks, and started back to our alpine meadow camp, in strong wind and rain.

I had noticed the amazingly different shades of blue and green deep down in the crevasses and ice-pools on the glacier and I was determined to film them as we finally left the camp and moved up with the last loads into the mountain world of rock and ice. After shooting a hundred feet or so of film I found that the filter was fogged with condensation and damp. I nearly wept with frustration, but cleaned it and filmed all the same sequences again. The result was, of course, that I got left behind and had to follow up after the others on my own. My load seemed very heavy as I staggered up the last moraine slope to where we had dumped our loads yesterday. That afternoon we climbed up into an area that really felt mountainous. There were scree slopes running down past towering rocks like ruined castles. Gradually the compass began to show that we were moving towards the west, even south-west at times, and away in the distance we could see the Smyth Channel from the ridge where we finally dumped the loads. It was pleasant to clamber back to the tents without loads on our backs and soon we were warm inside our sleeping bags, reading and chatting. Every half hour or so the sound of ice avalanches thundering down the icefall at the head of the glacier we had camped beside made us tense up and listen. Although we knew we were safe, we waited each time until the noise echoed around and died away. It was an eerie sensation listening to the avalanches, because the clouds were so low that we could not see them, only hear the sound booming around the cliffs.

The clouds were very low again when we set out after breakfast. My load seemed terribly heavy that day and my shoulders and back ached. The discomfort was not made any easier by the strong, blustering wind that kept blowing us off balance. An enforced rest was very welcome when Eric discovered he had left his balaclava on a rock and went back to fetch it. The kit bags we had left on the ridge the day before were soon located and I rearranged my loads to leave a lot of my wet clothes in the rucksack that also held the film stock. I was very worried about the film and hoped that damp had not got into any of the rolls. Cleaning my cameras was a job I had to discipline myself to do whenever there was a chance. One of the horrors of expedition filming is that one never sees the results until all the film has been exposed and one returns to Britain. At home the rushes are processed every few days and one can tell immediately if there were any faults with the camera, or a hair in the gate or the exposure has been wrong, and with luck, film those sequences again. Here in Patagonia I had to expose all 6,000 feet of film and hope that everything was all right. The first showing of the rushes eventually back in Britain is a nerve-racking business. One usually vows never to make a film again!

The next stage was extremely exhausting. The route led up and down scree, even over sheer mud walls of moraine and across glaciers covered with rocks, some as large as houses. It contoured round valleys, mainly on loose rock. As I felt so tired, the going seemed very difficult. At last we came to a col and below was a grassy valley with huge, erratic blocks littered about like giant dice, and lower down, a few trees. We found a sheltered spot surrounded on three sides by these towering blocks. Above us in the clouds we could see a dirty, hanging glacier streaked brown with grit, boulders and rock. There were enough trees around to provide us with firewood, but we had an early supper and were in bed by seven o'clock. The thought of having to go back the next day for the loads made us feel tired before we had started. But we were encouraged to find that our compasses showed we were beginning to move south. We were succeeding in circling Mount Burney.

I filmed quite a bit of the journey back the next day, after we had fetched the loads, but because of the fierce winds and sleet my hands became numb with cold. We tried a different, higher route, but it was far worse than the previous one. Halfway across the glacier an enormous ice avalanche came down a hanging glacier to our left, but because of my cold hands I had packed the camera away. I threw off my rucksack and scrabbled frantically for the camera, getting it out just in time to film the last dying seconds of the avalanche. I carried the camera in my hands for the rest of the journey, but not a single block of ice moved an inch. Such is documentary film making.

We climbed steeply up some snow and dropped our packs, while Eric and Jack hammered pieces off a steep outcrop of rock that turned out to be composed of tuff, as indeed was all the rock we had encountered. I filmed this scientific work! Sleet and rain forced us into our tents once we were back at the camp, and I set about cleaning and drying the film cameras. They seemed in good condition in spite of four nights of lying out in a rucksack.

One does not usually expect to have to cut steps with an ice-axe in hard mud, but on the next stage of our journey this is exactly what Eric had to do, before we could climb down the steep slope to the next glacier. Once on the glacier, we could see great hanging ice-cliffs and a lot of avalanche debris, so we trod particularly gently and apprehensively. The ice itself was very smooth and slippery and we had quite a job getting off at the far side.

We were soon passing below an enormous rock face with towers and buttresses. High above we could see a little brêche and we tried to reach it by climbing directly up, but the route led over smooth slabs covered in rock debris. We retreated and then thought that a gully might lead us down and around the obstacle, but that also proved too difficult. Feeling a little bewildered about the route, we descended to the wooded valley below and had lunch.

We decided to leave the loads here, as scrambling about on loose rock with seventy-pound rucksacks was not easy, and we then climbed up scree past the towers and bulges to the brêche. But this also turned out to be a bad move. It was extremely steep on the far side with a sheer drop of 1,000 feet to a little glacier below.

We retreated once again and kept searching for a way to get past the rock face without having to push and struggle through the thick forest below. Eventually we found a ledge just underneath the rock face itself. There were a couple of awkward moves, but with great relief we realised we had at last succeeded, and we had a quick look round the corner to see the route we would have to follow the next day.

As we returned to the rucksacks, there was a sudden clearing in the clouds and we had a fleeting glimpse of a steep ridge and even the summit covered in magnificent ice-flutings. It hung in space above us for a few seconds and was gone, as clouds and rain closed in once more.

It had been a long but significant day. It was the first time that we had had to do any rock climbing, albeit for short sections, but we had at last begun to swing south, even south-east. It looked as if we were reaching the end of the mountain.

The rain drummed on the tent all night and still continued into the morning. We had had an early breakfast but we stayed put in our sleeping bags because of the bad conditions. I had a book of modern British poetry with me and passed the time trying to learn "Welsh Landscape" by R. S. Thomas. It was nostalgically evocative and I could see in my mind the Welsh hills and hear the gentle lilt of some of my hill-farming friends. Happy days spent in the Welsh mountains and cottages flooded through my memory.

By eleven the rain had eased and we packed the soaking tents and set off. The lull was short-lived and soon it was raining hard again. With a full waterproof suit on I sweated

47

really hard and soon was soaked with a mixture of sweat and the rain running down my neck. It was terribly enervating and the continual up and down with scrambling on loose rock made us feel exhausted. After a while it started to snow and we climbed on in a blizzard and thickening cloud. I filmed a lot of this, but once again my hands became numb with cold.

We reached the ledge below the rock face with the bulges and towers. The route across, which we had followed yesterday, looked pretty unpleasant. Two streams were now flowing across it and wet snow made the going treacherous. We roped ourselves together but all went well and we reached our furthest point of yesterday, beyond the scree.

I suppose it was tiredness, youthful inexperience and arrogance, but my diary shows a distinct bout of ill-temper on my part.

Jack wanted to go down a gully and into the forest. My diary says: "I *knew* there was a way round at the foot of the rock face, so I just went and they followed." It was a behaviour pattern I was to experience from other people, sixteen years later in Tierra del Fuego.

It was turning out to be a bad day for Jack. The wind began to blow really fiercely and kept knocking us over again and again, as it caught us off balance. The huge loads made a much larger area for the wind to catch. As we climbed up an awkward scree, Jack's load fell off and rolled down for over a hundred feet, nearly disappearing in a gully. We recovered it while Eric silently plodded on, with his enviable methodical rhythm.

More loose scree was followed by an area of tufted grass and stunted bushes. A boulder the size of a football dislodged itself from above and rolled, bouncing higher and higher every few feet, towards Jack. He saw it just in time and warded it off with his ice-axe, like a cricketer slipping an awkward ball away to leg. There was a sharp crack and we saw that the shaft of his ice-axe had broken.

We eventually found a camp site in a windy place below a high, black, over-hanging cliff, above which was a steep

Above: Eric in 1963.

Right: Eric taking his turn at carrying the rubber inflatable boat weighing 150 pounds, but essential to our progress towards Mount Burney.

Puerto Olla, our landing point to approach Monte Bové, with the Beagle Channel and Devil's Island in the distance.

The first ascent of Monte Bové, 1963: *above*, our camp on the South Face, looking out over the lower ranges of Tierra del Fuego; *left*, Eric during the ascent; *below*, the summit, Claudio Cortez, the author and Eric Shipton.

glacier that released huge blocks of ice in thundering cascades every half hour.

The tents were completely soaked as we put them up and leaking a constant stream of drips on us, as we crawled into our soggy down sleeping bags. Inside the tents it was like being in a dank cave, and our breath steamed in the candle-light. It was still pouring with sleet and rain driven by a shrieking wind off the Pacific.

Jack had a splendid characteristic that made him pretend that even when everything went wrong, it was exactly what he meant to happen or do. He almost made us believe that the best way to get his load down the mountain was to drop it and roll it down. Of course he had meant to break his ice-axe warding off the rock. It was pretty useless anyway and it must have had a weak shaft.

That night in our steaming tents he was determined to dry out his sleeping bag a little over the Primus. Each time he attempted to do this he got it too close to the flame. The cover blackened and the tent was filled with the stench of burning feathers. Flapping and patting at the smoking bag, he managed to avoid actual flames leaping up. "That's right," he said, "that will dry it well. Just what I meant to do. Must be a very poor material." Once again he held the bag over the stove and once again the smell of scorching filled the tent. "Very good," he said. "That's it, Well done." I remember rocking and aching with silent laughter; I should have hated to offend him. No, it was not Jack's day.

Almost unbelievably the storm went on all night. We had tried to sleep at eight and I had dropped off, but woke at twelve shaking with wet and cold. As so often when one has taken the edge off sleep and tiredness, I could not get to sleep again and lay listening to the gusts shaking the tent until after four. I suppose I finally dropped off, but awoke again at seven. It was still snowing and hailing.

We had the misery of getting into wet clothes, soaking socks and boots and cold, damp waterproofs that morning. The outer edges of my hands at the base of the little fingers had deep open cracks caused by being continually wet. They stung and ached as I tied up the laces of my boots.

In fact, once we got moving it was great fun in the snow, as we climbed over the col to fetch the loads we had left out all night. When we reached them I took out the cameras to film some incongruous-looking red flowers poking through the snow and I had that deep hollow feeling of despair. The cameras were running with water. The exposure meter was soaking too, and would not work. I trudged back to camp swearing blindly with rage at the weather, the mountain, the route, anything on which I could vent my anger.

In my tent I set to work to dry the cameras as best I could and check the film stock. Water was actually swilling around in one camera and the film inside had snapped and was ruined. The polythene bags in which everything had been wrapped seemed almost to attract water by some capillary action, and it had seeped in through any little holes there were. One roll of exposed film was completely ruined and another two looked very damp. My stills camera was also full of water and the shutter was not working correctly. This was a bad day for *me*.

I had to leave most of the sorting and drying out to do later, as it was vital to move on with a load that afternoon. We had set out from the lake originally with eighteen days' food with us. We had now been on our journey for ten days and as we had no idea how much longer it was likely to take us to return to the food dump left by the boat, Eric had put us on half rations.

It snowed on and off for the rest of that day and as well as splendid shots I could have got in the swirling snow, there were impressive views of a towering ice fall. But of course no camera was operating. As if to rub it in even more, away to the west there was a brilliant shimmer on the sea under dark, black, storm clouds.

It took me three and a half hours to dry out the cameras that night but at least when I had finished they still worked.

A lot of new snow lay on the long slopes up to the col. The weather was better and, far away beyond the amazing green and blue seracs of the icefall, we could just see a peak which could only be Tryfan One. It was a moment of great excitement and a feeling of achievement. We were now heading east and our route-finding had been absolutely correct. With nothing to go on but a very inaccurate map we had clambered up and down countless glaciers and ridges radiating from Mount Burney like the spokes of a wheel, and had now ended up at the head of the right valley to take us back down to the plain.

The good weather did not last and within minutes it was snowing hard and the clouds had come right down. We groped blindly on and realised that the ground was steepening sharply. We sat and waited, and when it cleared a little we saw that we were on the edge of a sheer drop down to a glacier that had a river running from it towards the plain. We had nearly walked off the cliff. When it cleared enough to see where one was going, Jack set off to find a way down. It was a steep slope of mud, rocks and – surprisingly – wild flowers. We had to rope up for one difficult section, made more difficult by cascades of sleet streaming down the rock, but we reached the river at last and put up the tents for the night.

We lay low during the morning of the next day as rain and sleet pounded down on the tents. Eric brought the Primus across to mine to warm it up a little and to dry the sleeping bags. We tried not to emulate Jack's method! After a quick lunch we brought down the loads from above, and then set off on a reconnaissance to try to find a way across the glacier.

After several false attempts we succeeded in traversing the glacier by twisting and turning through a maze of crevasses. High above us, half hidden in the clouds, we could make out an incredible line of ice-cliffs and a broad icefall. It was a remarkable size for such a small mountain; Mount Burney is only 5,700 feet. Eric compared it to a Karakorum icefall, not only for size but also the weird, pointed ice-pinnacles and spires that towered up into the grey, streaming clouds.

When we got back to camp Eric moved his Li-lo and soaking sleeping bag across from his wedge tent to mine. His tent had been especially designed for him. While the shape was good from the point of view of presenting only a small area of wind resistance, there were other faults that made it not very satisfactory. My tent was the well-tried and splendid Meade, but of course that was designed for high altitude and cold snow conditions rather than incessant rain. Both tents were leaking badly by now.

It was a hell of a night. The wind howled and lashed the rain at the already sodden tents. I went out at about ten thirty to deal with the guys on both tents and got even more soaked than I had been.

Eric and I were both woken at two by a crack of wind that nearly took the tent away, and this time it was Eric who staggered out into the pitch dark to deal with the pegs which had been torn out of the ground. We both slept fitfully for the rest of the night in our cold, clammy down bags.

The wind had dropped a little by the morning, but it was still raining. We cooked breakfast lying in our sleeping bags, taking it in turns to hold the Primus on our laps trying to dry the bags out a little. Muffled curses and groans came from the solitary Jack, a few yards away in the wedge tent. Through his splendid, spluttering sardonic rage came the information that a stream was actually running though the tent; in one side and out the other. He seemed to think that he was in danger of floating off on his Li-lo on a wild, white water ride into the river.

We cramponed our way eventually across the glacier and, with a short spell of step-cutting, I led down to the moraine. Soon we were by the river and the lake and on to thick grass – lush, green meadows with forests on the far side. The contrast and the delight it brings is always more pronounced after days, sometimes weeks, up in the high world of rock, ice and snow. Man belongs, I suppose, more to this familiar world, than the rarer world of mountains and feels more at home in the safe and known surroundings.

We could sit together by a morale-boosting wood fire, something we had not done for two weeks, and eat a huge meal. We were back now on full rations. Away in the distance we could hear avalanches rumbling down the icefall. We felt very happy and contented. We had not climbed

Mount Burney and I know Jack felt sad about this and, in a strange way, I too felt slightly cheated. But Eric was obviously pleased with the journey round the mountain. We had done what we set out to do and had discovered and explored a lot of unknown ground and glaciers. We knew the shape of Mount Burney and had a good idea of its composition, and I had made a pretty good film of an area of the world where no man had ever been before.

But, of course, it was a false relaxation. We still were a very long way from civilisation and we had a hard and dangerous journey ahead of us. It took us three hours to push through the forest to the plain with our first load. It was just over three weeks since we left Punta Arenas and we had completed the circle in twelve days. The humid forest made us all feel very tired as we wallowed about through the fallen tree trunks covered in moss and lichen. There were several little streams and deep, swampy gullies to cross. Some of the film I shot of this section really showed what Darwin meant when he described the forests of this part of the world as "temperate jungle".

Jack had stayed in bed the following day with a bad headache and Eric and I set off back towards the icefall to get some rock samples and for me to film him at work. It was very enervating again and I felt drained. The 1960s were the early days of nylon garments waterproofed with PVC, and British Nylon Spinners had given us waterproofs free to test for them. Our suits were highly efficient at keeping out water, but of course one became soaked in sweat, despite generous ventilation vents, and I felt sure this contributed to the lassitude and feeling of exhaustion we all experienced from time to time.

Eventually, it was time to leave this most beautiful of all our camp-sites, with the forest on one side and, beyond the meadows and lake, the great icefall towering up towards the summit of Mount Burney; indeed, the whole end of the valley was filled by this view.

The loads seemed cripplingly heavy and once again I was ranging about like a demented sheep dog, trying to film the

53

progress through the forest. I would get left behind and then rush and fall in my efforts to catch up with the others. I had accepted this on the mountain but here, in the forest, it seemed to pull me down as it had not done before. Of course it was a nuisance for the other two as well. When one is tired, one does not want to stop and wait and start again, losing all the rhythm of movement. They were probably cursing and swearing at me as much as I was secretly and silently cursing them. However, we reached the plain amicably but very tired, and that was when the most ironic and frustrating thing happened. The weather cleared and we suddenly had our first clear view of Mount Burney, a great rock peak covered in verglas, and behind, an easy-looking snow dome. The great peak hung in space above the forest, glowing with the last rays of the sun, and slowly the stars came out in a cold, clear sky. We could almost hear the mocking laughter.

5

The first ascent of Mount Bové

For me, the anticipation of getting back to civilisation always seems to outweigh the possible feeling of anti-climax of the return journey. But I also always have a strong reluctance to leave the wild parts of the world. There is always so much more to be done. Each expedition merely paves the way for others, and on this one we had not climbed Mount Burney.

When we reached our lakeside dump and came to inflate the RFD we found both pumps had perished and we had to blow it up by mouth. Our lives depended on getting that boat blown up. We each took three- or four-minute turns, at the end of which we reeled away feeling giddy and sick. Eric with his "high-altitude" lungs seemed able to manage longer spells, and after another hour the boat appeared hard enough to launch in the lake.

Mercifully the engine fired first time. But all this only emphasised Eric's earlier statement, which I had not really credited, that this was in some ways the most dangerous expedition that he had ever been on. He felt that we were more out on a limb than in many of his previous trips, including Everest and the Himalayas.

Jack was, I realised at the time, and indeed confirmed sixteen years later, bitterly disappointed with the expedition and felt that it had been a complete waste of energy and resources. Eric, on the other hand, had delighted in the exploration which seemed to Jack just pottering about, in this remote and testing countryside. I am sure he was saddened by Jack's reaction. In any event our journey round Mount Burney had strengthened us considerably and got Eric and me into excellent trim for our next expedition.

Ever since I had read about Darwin and the voyage of the *Beagle* with Captain Fitzroy, I had wished to visit that amazing stretch of water that cuts through from the Pacific to the Atlantic, and that is named after his little boat, the Beagle Channel, and now was my chance. Eric had seen mountains lying at the eastern end of the peninsula from the summits of the peaks in the Darwin Range which he had climbed in 1962. As with much of the rest of the range, this group was largely unexplored and it was to be the objective of our second trip this year. Jack Ewer was unable to stay on, and made his way back to Santiago. We were now joined by Peter Bruchhausen, an Argentine geophysicist who had been with Eric in Patagonia three years before, and Claudio Cortez, a young rock climber and medical student from Santiago. Eric liked the idea of taking representatives from the countries in which he climbed with him on his expeditions and Claudio filled this role.

The Chilean navy acts as a transport system in this region with its thousands of miles of coastline, not only for the various naval bases on the islands but for remote and outlying estancias as well, and an interview with the admiral in charge of the third Chilean naval zone secured our passage. Our six-day rest in Punta Arenas raced by and on February 12th we had to readjust to setting off once more. Facing up to the hardships of a second expedition so soon after the first is more difficult than setting out first time. One drops back so quickly into the soft life. I found myself reluctant to leave Mrs. Stewart's cooking and comfortable beds and baths, but it was not long before Eric's quiet enthusiasm swept me along to anticipate this new trip eagerly.

The docks were a busy hustle of ships loading and unloading. Antiquated cranes ran on rails up and down the quay and dockers heaved and hauled the huge loads of fertiliser and wool on and off the ships. On the west side were two naval vessels: one the *Lientur*, which had transported Eric on his ice-cap crossing and the other a squat, ocean-going tug, the *Cabrales*, which was to take us now. The decks of this little boat were alive with sailors and civilians loading hay, sacks of onions, planks, drums of oil and other supplies. Our fellow passengers included a collie, two little boys, an estancia owner, some naval personnel and Father Stockin, a Catholic priest visiting outlying parishes.

At two o'clock precisely the captain arrived looking very British in his naval uniform and I later discovered that the Chilean navy is modelled very much on the Royal Navy and there has always been a feeling of great friendship between the two. He saluted the quarter-deck in proper fashion and within moments we were slipping away from the busy port and its clutter of ships, including a sailing cargo ship, and then down into the Magellan Straits. A steel-hulled, four-masted barque lay anchored off the city. It was used for storing coal, but it added a touch of Conradesque romance to the scene. Looking back from a few miles out we could see that Punta Arenas lay just along the shore and for a short way up the hill behind and that was all; beyond stretched the forest and the wilderness. It was surprising to see how remote and cut off this city of 40,000 people looked.

It was warm and fine as we steamed south-west and soon dolphins began to roll over and over in the bow wave. We were invited to the bridge to meet the captain, who did not speak much English, but several of his young officers did and we were able to establish a very friendly rapport with him and his crew by the time we had reached Puerto Harris on Dawson Island.

This was a Chilean naval base but it used to be an important centre for boat-building, mainly cutters, and some

5,000 people used to live on the island. In 1963 only 500 were stationed there and they were mainly naval personnel. We went ashore in the long boat and visited the little church with Father Stockin. When we returned to the *Cabrales* it was time for supper, and soon after we clambered into our narrow bunks in the hot, juddering depths of the ship.

I woke several times in the night wondering where I was, with sweat running down my face and neck. It was desperately hot in our cabins. At seven o'clock we were called on deck to look at Mount Sarmiento, a beautiful ice-spire thrusting up through a bank of low mist. It was a well-known landmark for the early navigators of the Magellan Straits and many of the old grain and wool clippers used to sight this peak, as it marked the entrance to the straits when coming from Australia. It had been climbed by Father de Agostini, an Italian priest who had visited the Darwin Range with Italian guides and had made several first ascents there. This was the start of the mountains now, and in the calm, clear weather we could see snow peaks in the distance, while nearer, the coastline was very like the Western Isles of Scotland.

Our voyage took on a distinctly civilised air as we sipped our aperitifs with the captain before lunch, but soon afterwards, we moved out of the shelter of the innumerable islands and met a heavy Pacific swell that made the little *Cabrales* pitch and roll in a most uncivilised way. The visibility dropped, as low banks of drizzle rolled in from the west, and the young naval cadets on board had a busy time taking compass bearings and navigating in this labyrinth of channels and islands that forms the incredible southern Chilean coastline.

The weather suddenly cleared again and we swung back towards the east and entered the Beagle Channel. This historic stretch of water ranges from five miles to one mile wide, and nearer to us now were tall peaks and huge glaciers that ran to the water's edge. At the western end of the Beagle Channel there are deep, forested fiords cutting back into the mountains both north and south from the channel. It was an

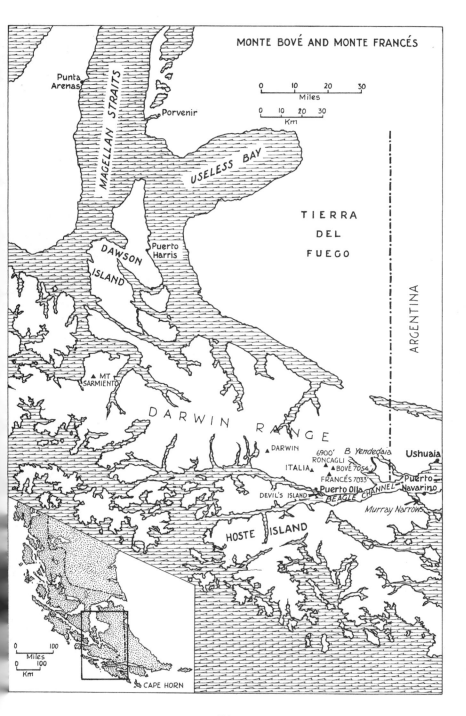

MONTE BOVÉ AND MONTE FRANCÉS

Punta Arenas
Porvenir

MAGELLAN STRAITS

USELESS BAY

0 10 20 30
Miles

0 10 20 30
Km

TIERRA

DEL

FUEGO

ARGENTINA

DAWSON ISLAND

Puerto Harris

MT SARMIENTO

D A R W I N   R A N G E

DARWIN

6900' B. Yendegaia
RONCAGLI
ITALIA ▲ BOVÉ 7054' Ushuaia
FRANCÉS 7033'
DEVIL'S ISLAND Puerto Olla Puerto Navarino
BEAGLE CHANNEL
Murray Narrows

HOSTE ISLAND

0 100
Miles
0 100
Km

CAPE HORN

59

exciting and inspiring sight, as the sun slipped down behind the peaks to the west, leaving the snow mountains and glaciers glowing as though lit by some internal red light. The *Cabrales* slid into Garibaldi Sound to anchor for the night, as we had our evening meal of fresh mussels, washed down by excellent Chilean wine.

My eulogising had come too soon. Dawn was bleak and cold with sleet and rain streaming out of low clouds. In my waterproofs I stood on the deck and filmed the black precipices of the Beagle Channel running with water, and the snout of the Italia Glacier that plunged out of the grey clouds and mist straight into the water in one gigantic icefall. We could not see the mountains we had come to explore as the clouds were down to 700 or 800 feet.

The captain took the *Cabrales* into a small bay called Puerto Olla, on the northern side of the Beagle Channel near the divide of the north-west and south-west arms. One of the cadets was up in the bows heaving the lead as we slid gently in through the grey rain-pocked waters. I could imagine Fitzroy edging the longboats of the *Beagle* into the same bay on his extraordinarily precise surveying voyages. Many of the charts of the area state that they are based on the original survey of Fitzroy with only a few modern corrections. With the glimmer of a smile of satisfaction, and this was the first time I had seen him smile, the captain called for the anchor to be dropped and the *Cabrales* came to a standstill in the sheltered bay. It was the first time a Chilean naval vessel had been in here.

They lowered the long boat, and all our gear and food, as well as the RFD rubber dinghy, the outboard and twenty gallons of petrol were packed into it, and in the cold drizzle they rowed us ashore. As we passed along the side of the little tug the captain and his officers and cadets lined the deck; they did not smile or even wave. Was it imagination or did I detect the same mixture of pity and disbelief on their faces as I had seen on the faces of the peons when they had left us on our journey to Mount Burney? With a rather strangled toot on the siren, the *Cabrales* slipped away through the slanting drizzle and out into the steel-grey, wind-whipped Beagle Channel. We were on our own.

A great wall of dripping forest rose up from the beach and we saw at once why other expeditions, hearing about this supposedly impenetrable "temperate jungle", had not attempted to climb in these mountains, except Father de Agostini and one Argentine expedition. As we moved all the equipment and food into a delightful dell, we came across the remains of a* wooden wigwam, probably left there years before by the Yahgan Indians who used to collect mussels and hunt in these waters. At the same time the weather cleared and the whole scene was transformed. We could see Olla Bay fully now, a half mile crescent of sand backed by the forest, almost encircling the turquoise blue waters of the lagoon. Brown fronds of kelp waved languidly in the gentle swell and a pair of kelp geese swam along the shores. A sea-lion poked its inquisitive head out of the water and watched us with huge, brown, limpid eyes and twitching whiskers. It was very warm, and the sun shone brightly from a blue sky. An hour ago it had been grey and cold with steady rain. It brought home very forcibly how unpredictable and change-able was the weather of West Tierra del Fuego.

It was low tide and we collected a billy-can full of mussels, cooked them over a wood fire and ate them for breakfast. We all felt a great reluctance to leave this idyllic spot, but eventually we started inland on the reconnaissance, carrying supplies for seven days.

Eric's plan had now resolved itself. Father de Agostini had visited the area and climbed a peak which he named Monte Italia. An Argentine expedition had attempted Monte Bové from the east and had failed because of bad weather and a difficult approach. With the three peaks that Eric had climbed in 1961 and, of course, Sarmiento, climbed by de Agostini's party, this was the only climbing and exploration that had been carried out in an area the size of the European Alps. A map in de Agostini's book, *Sfingi di Chiaccio*, had made it look as if it was possible to reach the Western Face of Bové from the head of the Italia Glacier, the one we had seen in the mist-shrouded dawn on our arrival and which lay to the west of Olla Bay. Eric now wished to follow this route to Bové.

Without wasting another minute we set off, pushing through the thick forest until we reached a fast-flowing, glacial stream, milky white, rushing rapidly along, deep down in a gully cut into soft, forest soil. It was too deep, fast and cold to wade but luckily a fallen tree trunk made a natural bridge. Peter Bruchhausen, our Argentine geophysicist, crawled across while I filmed him and then we hauled the loads across. Trying to speed up the process, I threw my ice-axe in an attempt to get it to the other side. It whirled in an arc, hit the branch of a tree and disappeared into the stream. Cursing my stupidity, I spent a very cold quarter of an hour wading about in my underpants, feeling with my feet for the axe. Luckily, just as the intense pain from the icy water was numbing my feet and legs, I felt it with my toes and grabbed it quickly before it was washed any further down stream. That moment of unthinking behaviour could have jeopardised the whole expedition, for we carried no spares and I could not have climbed high on to the glaciers and snow fields of the Darwin Range without it.

After another tedious stretch of forest, where we floundered about over fallen trees and closely-packed trunks, with our packs getting caught on low branches, we emerged on to a ridge and were delighted to find a broad, well-defined track running up the mountain. It wound through the forest and soon we climbed out above the tree line at nearly 1,000 feet. We knew that nobody lived near here. The Indians were long since dead, and we could only guess that the track had been made by guanaco on their way to high pastures.

The weather had become changeable again and there were sudden rain squalls followed by bright sun. Brilliant rainbows shone across the Beagle Channel and Devil's Island, now 3,000 feet below us. We cut through many rock bluffs and false summits and gradually the track petered out as the vegetation grew less. I was plodding on with my head down when I suddenly heard a great rush of air and a strange whistling and swishing noise. I jerked up as a huge shadow flashed across and I saw a condor wheeling over me about thirty feet away. We had seen these birds on Mount Burney but never as close as this. I could see the white ruff around the neck, the folds of the turkey-like neck and the fingers of the feathers outspread at the wing tips. With a wing span of ten feet or more it was an awesome sight and the wind made a thrumming noise in its feathers, like a glider, as it swooped over us once more. These condors were to become our constant companions whenever we moved on the lower slopes of the mountains.

At seven thirty Eric, Claudio and I reached a small level plateau at about 4,000 feet and decided to pitch a camp. We had an Arctic Pyramid tent that, even when dry, weighed a total of sixty pounds. Eric had used one before, both on the ice-cap and here on the Darwin Range, for he believed that even the best mountain tents of that time would not stand up to the ferocious hurricanes of this mountain range, only seventy miles from Cape Horn. When sledging in the Antarctic it is, of course, an easy matter to fold the tent up like an umbrella with the poles still in position and tie it on to the sledge. Here in the Darwin Range we had to dismantle it completely each time we took it down, and pack it away in its bag. This did not take too long, as it was a simple tent and superbly strong; its weight was its only drawback.

Soon we were snugly installed and sat waiting for Peter Bruchhausen. After an hour we became worried as he had not appeared and Eric and I descended back down the way we had come to look for him. He had last been sighted only a few hundred feet below. We wandered about calling in the gathering dusk and rain, fearing that he might have missed the camp-site. We had no luck, and with mounting fears returned to the tent. Meanwhile Claudio Cortez, who had been ranging about on a level with the camp, suddenly stumbled upon Peter lying on a ledge only a few hundred yards away. He was half conscious and apparently had been having severe bouts of vomiting, during which he must have passed out. After discussion we reckoned that he must either have been allergic to mussels or had eaten a bad one at our early morning breakfast on the beach. He was obviously feeling very weak, so we led him back to the tent in worsening weather; it had been a lucky escape.

The wind increased all night and it started to snow. I had to crawl into some waterproofs and put on my boots in order to clamber out at three a.m. to tighten the guys. My previous similar escapades on Mount Burney had strengthened my resolve for this work and I was soon back in my bag to sleep soundly until eight o'clock.

The wind was still blowing snow with a gentle, soft, hissing noise onto the tent but inside the Pyramid we were warm and comfortable, its merits were becoming more apparent every minute. We lay and read and chatted until lunchtime and then dressed fully before setting out at one thirty to clamber first up the ridge and then down a gully to a glacier that was not shown on the map. We tied ourselves together on the climbing rope, as there were a large number of crevasses and the visibility was not good in the blowing powder snow. I was in the lead at this stage and I zig-zagged up towards the bergschrund. A simple snow bridge spanned the gaping chasm and I moved easily, before tackling the steep ice beyond. I had cut some twenty or thirty steps in near-vertical ice when we all realised that it was going to take a very long time to reach the distant col by this route, so we retreated off the glacier. We were all rather bewildered by trying to base our exploration on what Father de Agostini had written in his book and on his map, which appeared most inaccurate. Admittedly, the visibility had been poor and we had not seen the interior of the range, but it was hard to discover which route the priest and his Italian guides had followed.

We had another very warm snug night. The security of the Pyramid tent was excellent for giving the feeling of a team working together. We were all there in the one tent. We ate together, we planned together and we dozed together. There was none of the loneliness I had felt when I had been on my own in my tent on Mount Burney and I suddenly realised that, though I was not a normally gregarious person, I had

Climbing towards the summit of Monte Francés.

The huge icefall of the Italia Glacier plunges into the Beagle Channel.

The East Face of Monte Francés, largely unmapped in 1963.

missed the companionship of the others on that trip.

It was still sleeting as we set off after breakfast down the gully to the glacier. As we reached the ice we heard a shrill whinnying and saw four guanaco galloping in what appeared to be almost slow motion on their long thin legs, up the steep moraine slope. They paused on the sky line and looked down their noses at us, blinking their long eyelashes. They made a good film sequence. We never saw so many together again but we stumbled a few times on a solitary creature.

We struck a good line up the glacier and reached the col we had seen yesterday. We then scrambled on loose rock and scree up a gully, to emerge on to a high glacial plateau. Away below us to the left we could see the huge icefall of the Italia Glacier that plunged eventually into the Beagle Channel. One exceptionally strong gust caught Peter Bruchhausen off balance and blew him ten feet on to a soft snow bridge which promptly gave way, leaving him hanging with his legs wildly kicking over the icy depths of the crevasse. We hauled him out and tottered on our way towards the north-east.

We could see the lower slopes of Monte Italia disappearing up into the cloud, but when at about 5,800 feet we reached a col that led down to the vast Roncagli Glacier, there was no sign of Monte Roncagli. Instead we were confronted with the sheer rock face of Monte Francés some 2,000 feet, covered in ice fluting and verglas. Quite obviously, no easy route could be found up such an awesome face as that, and in Tierra del Fuego you look for the easy ways first.

We ate our cheese and biscuits with the cold gnawing at our bones, feeling a little disappointed and rather cheated. We had come the wrong way, but at least we had discovered this early on, so had wasted only a few days on this abortive reconnaissance. In this we were lucky because, as Eric pointed out, the surrounding country could be shrouded in mist for weeks on end, or one could be prevented from moving at all by appalling weather. Route-finding in this unexplored mountain range can be a long and frustrating business.

There was nothing for it but to retrace our steps down

the glacier, with sudden onslaughts of wind grabbing and pushing at us, whirling the powder snow up in stinging clouds that peppered our bare faces like shot. In a steep little gully, Peter, who was leading, slipped and started to slide down at an ever-increasing speed. I struck wildly with the point of my ice-axe into the hard snow and by some incredible fluke it held. The rope between us tightened and twanged like an elastic band and Peter came to a halt, but the shock had been too much for my balance and it was now my turn to shoot off down the steep slope. My mountaineering reflexes worked and I rolled over on to my front and pulled myself up with a classic ice-axe brake. It is odd how one reacts to near-serious accidents. Peter and I stood up and howled with laughter, as if it was the funniest thing that had ever happened to us and then went careering off down the next snow slopes with gay abandon. We reached the tent at eight o'clock. We had been on the move for ten hours on a significant but frustrating part of the expedition.

It was no wonder we slept late the next day, but we had soon packed up camp and set off back down to Puerto Olla along the guanaco track. We arrived in a couple of hours and Eric and I boiled a full billy-can of mussels which we ate with delight. Moules marinières à la Beagle – we made sure Peter did not have any!

As we had the RFD inflatable with us we pumped it up. By now the pumps had dried out and were working again. I suddenly had the mental image of Jack dancing up and down on them a couple of weeks ago and wished he was with us. I think he would have enjoyed the challenge of this mountain range much more than he had Mount Burney. Eric and I were soon back to the old routine of packing everything into the dinghy. The engine started without a falter and within a few minutes we had set off across the bay to land on a very pleasant sandy beach on the far side. The forests here face towards the west and the trees have been blown by the strong prevailing winds into weird shapes and slants, very like trees one finds on the cliffs of North Devon and Cornwall; wedge-shaped and leaning away from the ever-present winds.

Only a few minutes after we had landed Eric suggested we did a quick reconnaissance to spy out the route for getting up into the mountains. He never wasted a minute. He had this lovely quality that always wants to see over the hill to what lies beyond the next horizon. He and I climbed easily through the forest on to a marshy plain that lay beside the Francés Glacier, to see if there was a route that led to the rocky, broken country higher up. The glacier flattened out here towards Puerto Olla but did not quite reach the Beagle Channel. It was a broad area of chaotic open crevasses and sérac some two miles wide and three miles long, to the foot of the icefall that plunged in a frozen cascade for over 1,000 feet from the high glacial plateau. We stood in silence and looked, each planning a possible route to avoid the glacier. When we eventually spoke to compare thoughts we were both agreed on the route for the morrow. With that marvellous binding of companionship that comes with sharing knowledge and skill in the wild, lonely places of the world, we strode quickly back to Peter and Claudio. We soon had a blazing fire going and set up camp in a beautiful glade. It was another outstanding place. Through the trees we could see the blue waters of the Beagle Channel flaked with white streaks in the steady wind, and beyond it the unknown peaks of Hoste Island. The close-crowded forest was all around us, but through the trees we could glimpse the white sparkling towers of the Francés Glacier and we knew that, still hidden from us, beyond and higher up, were the peaks we hoped to climb. We were on the threshold of our adventure.

I do not think that it was the anticipation of the unknown, but I could not sleep that night. I am a person who has always needed sleep and I am inclined to get neurotic if I do not get my full ration. I lay with my mind whirling, trying not to disturb the others, for we lay packed tightly together in the Pyramid tent. I cursed my inability to drop off, expecting I would feel tired and weak the next day. Quite a few people feel acute hypochondria on expeditions, rather in the same way as highly-trained athletes worry about every minor ache and pain. It would be very easy to brood over the possibility of falling ill, or hurting oneself or, on this night, of not being able to sleep. In the event, my sleeplessness had no effect at all. In fact, quite the reverse. When we set off after a long sorting and packing session I felt very fit and was moving well.

The going was firm and we managed to keep our socks and boots dry and even the weather was fine. We crossed a shallow little valley which reminded me very much of some of the hidden valleys between Moel Siabod and Moelwyns in Wales, except that at the end of it the view was blocked by the icefall of the Francés Glacier. We had lunch in our Welsh Valley and then climbed steeply up, beginning to move out of the vegetation into the world of rock, ice and snow. Once again I heard the whistle of wind in feathers and saw five condors wheeling round above us. They came extremely low and I got some very fine close-up shots for the film, as they swirled around with their legs hanging down like aeroplane wing flaps. I believe the effect is the same. As they turned in the air we could see the broad, white band across their wings that is the distinctive marking of the condor.

We dumped our loads to look for a camp-site and soon found a level area by a small lake that would do very well. At the end of this shallow valley we could see across to the other side of the glacier some five miles away. The route up Monte Francés looked fairly easy from this side and my diary says: "I hope we can have a crack at it. No sign of Bové yet."

Of our two South American companions only Peter was fluent in English. As Eric and I were not at all proficient with our Spanish this tended to divide our team into two. It is always very difficult when one person cannot speak a language and it demands a constant effort to draw him into the conversation and make him feel part of the group. I suspect that poor little Claudio felt rather on his own. So much of the idle chatter and talk of an expedition is hardly worth translating, but it is this easy flow of talk and humour that binds a group together. The quick aside, the odd remark, the recalled memory, or the shared experience are the delights of an expedition and help the cohesive unit of friendship. While

Peter was almost part of this whole, it was obvious that Eric and I were very close, working together, enjoying each other's company and thinking alike on most of the major issues. I hope that I did not mock Claudio unkindly, but he had not much sense of humour, while I, on the other hand, found many things in life very amusing. Probably an infuriating characteristic, but I hope I have always known when to stop and keep quiet. For some completely unknown reason I had nick-named Claudio, 'Basingstoke'. It was impossible to explain to him in my very poor Spanish why I called him this, or even that Basingstoke was a town in southern England; it would not have helped. Eric also found this amusing. Poor Claudio became Basingstoke for the rest of the trip.

So it seemed natural that Eric and I should set off together on a reconnaissance when the mist cleared next morning, leaving Peter and Claudio behind. The wind was ferocious as we climbed straight up above the camp towards a rocky summit, and then on to a small glacier beyond. We reached the head of a cwm and a sudden blast of wind whipped my balaclava off my head. I saw it go sailing away and disappear for ever into the mist and blown snow. The valley steepened and we had to cut steps in the ice. It was obvious there was no way here to gain the high plateau that we knew lay beyond. We were now roped together and traversed across loose steep rock back to the ridge. The wind increased in strength. We were blown about on the loose rocks and fell over a great many times. Suddenly a huge stone came flying through the air, blown by the wind, and narrowly missed Eric, who watched it with bewilderment as it shot by. We kept traversing west now, until we were above the Francés Glacier, and looking down we could see a route to follow across the awkward, shifting moraine slopes, that would lead us north towards Monte Bové. To test the route we descended, and then worked our way along it back to the tent so that we should have a good idea of which way to go the following day. We arrived back at the tent just as the rain and mist returned.

This day had further strengthened the rapport between Eric and myself as we had carried out a difficult reconnaissance together in very tiring and trying weather conditions. The ground we had covered had been treacherous and unpleasant, but we had worked together, each one anticipating the other's moves and thoughts. There was never any doubt that Eric was the leader from every point of view and yet it was I who did most of the actual moving ahead. His gentle, calm appraisal of the problems seemed to be transmitted to me and I instinctively knew which way he thought was best, and we arrived at the same conclusions and the same decisions.

The unpredictable weather of Tierra del Fuego astounded us yet again, when we awoke next day to bright sun and blue sky. We packed the gear and tent, leaving four loads behind, and set off on the long traverse above the Francés Glacier to the moraine ridge. The mountains shone in a clear, vivid light. Away to the west were the long sweeping ice slopes of Monte Francés rising up beyond the icefall. From our height we were able to look down on the whole chaotic jumble of crevasses and séracs. It was almost impossible to get any idea of the scale but some of the crevasses, a deep turquoise blue, must have been hundreds of feet deep and the séracs, huge towers and spires of glittering ice as vast as cathedrals. Ahead of us, at last we saw Monte Bové, a huge mound of a mountain with a sheer rock face on the southern side, capped with a thick layer of ice-cliffs like icing on a cake. There appeared to be a possible route up the West Ridge. At the head of the Francés Glacier, where it must have dropped down to the Roncagli Glacier, there was a very beautiful small rock peak jutting out of the ice that we called the Fang.

It was a tremendous strain on our ankles as we traversed across the steep, loose slopes. The other three dropped down eventually on to some wet snow slopes, while I kept high above them to film their progress and also to film water gushing out of a little side glacier. The temperatures in the sun were well above freezing and everywhere was full of the sound of rushing, roaring water, cascading down the ice and rocks to the Beagle Channel. The condors, as many as eight of them at one time, wheeled in the cloudless blue sky.

We had not gained very much height until now, but at least we began to climb snow slopes and ice, on to the high plateau at about 5,000 feet. We found the going very easy here as there was an amazing lack of nevé and nearly all the surfaces were hard ice, and where there was snow, it was still frozen. On the flat glacier there were very few crevasses but we roped up and belayed each other over the obvious danger areas. As we moved towards the South Face of Bové the sun dropped behind Francés and we could feel the chill suddenly grip the air. We eventually found a flat area of the glacier, near an outcrop of rock, to pitch the tent. It was a desolate, exposed place but we had no choice. We took a lot of care digging the tent in, by putting snow on the valance, and by packing snow round the few pegs hammered into the ice. Then we made sure that the Pyramid was firmly and securely placed with some rocks from the outcrop. Before the frosts finally stilled the world into ice, we collected water from a little trickle, to avoid having to melt snow. Soon the friendly Primus was roaring and inside the tent it was snug and warm as we looked forward to our Horlicks meat bar, thickened with oats. The sun lingered on the ice-cliffs crowning Bové, diffusing them with a red glow. Away to the south, the lower hills of Hoste Island were clothed in a blue haze and the air crackled with cold under the clear sky.

At one thirty a.m. the wind suddenly increased to hurricane force and it continued all through the night. Sudden blasts, violent and demented, hurled themselves at the tent. One could hear them coming. Above the general continuous roar of the wind and rattle of powder snow on the tent, we were aware of a higher shrieking noise rapidly approaching over the glacier. We lay waiting for it to arrive, wondering if the tent would survive yet another onslaught. The sound was like an express train that arrives with a sudden explosion of noise; a blast that tears at your eardrums and envelops you completely. When dawn arrived at last, we decided to stay put, hoping there would be a lull. But instead of improving it grew worse, if such a thing was possible.

Eric and Peter both had to go out into the storm to obey the call of nature. Peeing is an easy matter, of course, as a plastic bottle can be used. but crapping is a different matter. The body has an ability to control a lot of its functions under adverse conditions, but sometimes there is no alternative. Both Eric and Peter must have had a cold, stinging experience crouching behind a nearby outcrop of rock in the fierce eddies of powder snow that whirled across the ice. I lay in the warmth and comfort of my sleeping bag and filmed their progress to and from the tent, through the tunnel door! They disappeared completely in the near white-out conditions, within a few yards and on their return I watched them leaning and bending almost double as they tottered step by step into the wind, having enormous difficulty walking against the full blast. All around them the powder snow blew in dense, swirling clouds driven parallel to the ground.

We decided to cut rations in half in case this appalling weather lasted several days. Our main supplies were still below at the dump by the little lake. We lay and read. It was hard to talk against the noise of the wind cracking and flapping the canvas. Eric with a twinkle in his eye reminded us of that classic remark of his, "Bedsores are the most likely injury on an expedition."

By next morning the storm was dying away, but with sudden gusts hitting out at us, like the death throes of a huge wounded animal. After breakfast I filmed the others as they crawled out of the tent into the flurries of snow. As we set off down to fetch the other loads the wind faded away completely. The storm was dead. It was marvellous to be out again after being cooped up in the tent for a day. We were like children let out of school early as we swung away quickly down the glacier and arrived at the old camp-site in two and a half hours.

But bedsore weather returned teasingly, maliciously, for two more days anchoring us to our glacial plateau, though we did manage to bring up our loads from the lake dump in one of the lulls. However, by the evening of the second day the clouds and swirling snow had vanished and we eagerly planned our ascent of Monte Bové. But when Eric, who had a built-in alarm clock, woke us at three thirty a.m. we looked out with a sinking feeling of disappointment, for outside the tent it was thick cloud and drizzle. What a change! At six forty-five we peered out again as we had our porridge breakfast. It was clearing fast and the wind had dropped right away. By ten forty-five we had prepared ourselves for a climbing day.

Looking back at what we took, compared to the sophisticated gear with which climbers bedeck themselves these days, I am still astonished. We had one Hauserlay 120-foot nylon rope. We each had a pair of crampons and an ice-axe. Eric and I both wore pyjama trousers as pants. I had a pair of climbing breeches, a woollen shirt over a string vest and a woollen sweater. I felt so enervated in my waterproof clothing that I wore a nylon anorak which again had been supplied by British Nylon Spinners for my first Himalayan expedition. It was not waterproof. Eric wore a Grenfell cloth anorak. I took my waterproof trousers but did not wear them. Claudio and Peter wore similar clothing underneath their waterproof suits. We carried food for the day, which comprised cheese, biscuits and sweets. That was all, except that, of course, I was burdened with my film cameras and film stock.

After our late start it did not seem as if we really could go for the summit; the weather was uncertain, with a lot of low cloud and rain showers. We climbed up easily to below the icefall, avoiding a cone of avalanche debris. Before we tackled the ice we had lunch and then put on our crampons and tied ourselves on to the climbing rope. We climbed steadily up the steep ice, twisting and turning through the séracs. Luckily the icefall was devoid of snow and the crampons bit into the hard ice with a satisfying crunch. Although the route was steep in places we moved quickly, often together, and were delighted to find such an easy way through the maze of crevasses and séracs. Many of the crevasses were full of water, for the temperatures were well above freezing, and they were the most amazing colours in their depths – green, blue, turquoise. It looked almost as if they were lit from below with hidden, bright-coloured lights.

We emerged from the icefall after three hours, and the clouds gathered round us. Ahead lay a long, steep snow slope disappearing into the gloom. I was in the lead at this time. I do not remember Eric asking me to lead but somehow there was an understanding between us and it was an automatic decision. I think also he wanted to see how Peter and Claudio managed to cope with crampons and steep ice climbing. For Claudio this expedition was his first venture on to ice and snow.

We soon reached the broad West Ridge of the mountain and our compass showed we were still going north so we turned east and climbed on into the mist, sensing, however, an improvement in the weather; most important of all it was still calm. The ridge gradually became a series of mounting ice bosses like gigantic cauliflowers made of ice crystals, balanced on a narrow crest, overhanging on either side. Each mound was twenty or thirty feet high with almost vertical sides. Though steep, the climbing was easy, as it was possible to kick steps in the feathers of ice and reach the summit of each hump. We gained some 500 feet over these fantastic formations. One after another they loomed above us in the clouds until we stood on the highest, the summit of Monte Bové, just about 7,054 feet.

To make sure this was really the summit, we continued along the ridge and within a few minutes the clouds parted and we saw that the narrow crest started to fall very steeply. On both sides we looked down a sheer drop of several thousand feet. To the north we could see a glacier far below, towards the east and beyond a rock ridge, the crevasses of the Stoppani Glacier. At the time I had no idea that sixteen years later I would be exploring these unknown glaciers. But I knew that Eric never looked at unexplored vistas without planning new expeditions.

As we stood on the summit, gusts of sleet stung our faces

and hands, but the clouds kept on lifting and then closing in again, almost as if the mountains were shouldering and shrugging them off. We kept on seeing tantalising glimpses of the area. For a while we saw Roncagli standing above a group of fine granite spires. It appeared to be slightly lower than Bové, and a difficult-looking mountain. In many ways I feel views from the tops of mountains, on such days as this are almost more exciting than on fine, cloudless days. Something of the magic and mystery remains.

Obviously I had been influenced by Eric's attitude to peak bagging. He felt that mountain exploration and travelling were far more important and the climbing of summits incidental. But in spite of this, I still felt a deep enjoyment and satisfaction of knowing that we were the first men ever to stand on the summit of Bové and I am sure Eric did too.

We had reached the summit at three p.m. and after half an hour we started down in worsening weather, following our tracks across the snow. I had filmed the ascent of Bové and Eric had several times insisted on taking the camera himself and including me in some of the shots. Our descent in the gloom made a good sequence. In the BBC's version of the film which was edited later that year, while Eric and I were both out of the country, they built up a great drama of our getting lost in a blizzard, on our way down. It was not true, of course, but it showed what could be done with skilful editing, dramatic music and a producer with a little imagination!

We descended easily and quickly by a better route down the icefall and were back in camp by six p.m. A seven-hour day. A first ascent. We drank gallons of tea and had our supper in great spirits. My diary for February 25th ends quite simply: "A good day."

6

Francés and the *Beagle*

Luck had been with us for our ascent of Bové. The next day dawned cold, and within a few minutes heavy flurries of snow were being blown by a strong wind against the tent. It was bedsore weather again. By about two o'clock I felt terribly shut in and restless so I dressed to go out. Once outside I felt much better and wandered round fetching water from the trickle that was, surprisingly, still flowing, tightening the guy ropes and shovelling snow from the back wall of the tent. It was still very cold and soon my damp socks were frozen. I also wanted to film some shots of the tent in blizzard conditions, so I was glad when a snow storm arrived and enabled me to do this until worsening conditions drove me back inside, where I clambered in, trying not to soak everything and everybody with the snow that was plastered on my clothing and boots. We brewed tea and read and slept. Then it was supper. The day dragged on.

This is the time on expeditions when rows can develop. Boredom, inactivity and often a lack of purpose can trigger it off. The way a man laughs, or sniffs or eats noisily often causes an inner seething resentment that can burst out in flashes of ill temper. As long as one is aware of it, then no harm can come, but so often small things grow out of all proportion. Probably because of my communication problem with Claudio, I found him a difficult person to get to know. I felt he was lazy, but of course he was slightly built and found load-carrying exhausting. In my opinion, he never seemed to share the little chores in camp and pull his weight; but, looking back, I am sure now that it was because he did not really understand what was expected of him. These minor points serve to illustrate how resentment can grow. The other problem that caused me to glower and to behave in a most unreasonable and childish manner, at least inwardly, was to do with the rations, one of the most frequent sources of expedition quarrels. It had been made quite clear that our ration for each helping of sugar, for tea or porridge or Horlicks was one level spoonful. Claudio had not grasped this and always took a heaped spoonful. I remember spluttering with inner fury over this. It seems so trivial a matter now, but at the time it got out of all proportion and I remember brooding over it for hours.

But I must not give the impression that this was an expedition of sullen, ill-tempered people glowering with inner resentment. The others may well have had their pet hatreds of things I did and the way I behaved. Outwardly, however, we got on very well, in spite of the language difficulties, and there was always the marvellous, calming contentment of Eric and his ability to talk about and discuss a whole range of subjects. For him, conversation was one of the delights of life. On this particular night I remember he talked about the Sherpas and his admiration for them, his friendship with many of them, especially Angtharkay, who was with him on many of his outstanding expeditions in the Himalayas. Eric also talked about his work as British Consul General in Kashgar, a post he was offered in 1940 after he had been forced by the outbreak of war to abandon his plans for further extensive exploration of the Karakorum. This was an aspect of his life I had never heard about and it was full of intriguing stories, many of which later appeared in his splendid autobiography *That Untravelled World*. How could petty sulks about sugar last long in the company of such a man?

Our next objective was to attempt Monte Francés, and so at five the next morning we took our usual first glimpse at the weather. It must have been a comic sight as four faces emerged from the tunnel door, like some multi-headed tortoise. On this day all popped back in again quickly. Low cloud hung over the glacier and flurries of snow whirled in from the west. In spite of this we still had breakfast at seven and in most unpromising conditions we set off towards Francés.

We started to climb easily up through a line of crevasses, but when we reached about 6,000 feet, it was obvious that we were not going to be able to climb Francés that day, as the visibility was getting worse and the wind increasing. So as not to waste the day, we struck north towards a nunatak, to the south-east of the small, shapely peak we had called the Fang. When we reached it, Eric spotted an incredible dyke of granite, intruding into gneiss and we climbed across to look at it. Though he had no academic qualifications as a geologist, Eric had a great interest and a very fine practical knowledge of this subject and was always collecting rock samples. There was a huge hollow in the snow on the lee side of the nunatak and we had lunch sheltering in it. There was also an ice-cave nearby that made good shots for the film, when I crawled inside and took pictures of the others as they walked past.

After lunch we dropped down to a col at the head of the Roncagli Glacier. The wind had reached hurricane force and we had a hard time battling against it, but from the col itself we had good views to the glaciers in the interior of the eastern part of the Darwin Range. All the peaks themselves were in the clouds that were scudding along just above our heads. I wish now I had taken more notice of this particular day of exploration, when I was planning my return to Tierra del Fuego sixteen years later.

The enormous winds were hurling powder snow in violent spirals as we sailed back up to the nunatak and returned to the camp on a compass bearing. We had not climbed Francés but we had found a link through from the Francés Glacier to the Roncagli Glacier; a day of useful exploration that delighted Eric.

The weather seemed to have developed a rhythm and, as

soon as we got back, it closed in again on us with by now all too believable fury. We had to spend another day reading, chatting and dozing. I read one of my books, *Pigeon Pie*, for the second time. I suppose everyone's taste is different when it comes to books to take on an expedition. I like something that is easy to read, preferably with a good story and usually a touch of nostalgia or a reminder of Europe or Britain. Laurie Lee's *Cider with Rosie* is the sort of book I consider ideal for expeditions. I have also found that anthologies of poetry give me great comfort. On my first trip to the Himalayas I read Gerald Durrell's *My Family and Other Animals*. I lay in my tent weeping with laughter, so much so that the Sherpas thought I had gone mad with altitude and fear, and gathered outside the tent to listen to me! John Hillaby's walks through Britain and Europe have delighted me on expeditions in recent years and all the John Masters yarns of India have given me the strong story line I need. Later that night I became aware in moments of waking that the weather was improving. But we couldn't get properly under way until about one forty p.m., a late start for an attempt on an unclimbed summit. As we climbed, it became a day of startling beauty. The snow was frozen and crisp and our crampons bit well, as we scrunched upwards on an easy route through the séracs. The glaciers and icefalls of Monte Francés were wreathed in swirling mists that were lifting rapidly. Eddies of wind blew powder snow in glittering cascades across the hard surface, catching the sun that slanted in over a shoulder of Francés from a blue sky. It was quickly becoming the sort of day of which mountaineers dream. Behind us we could see Bové, the mountain we had climbed three days ago and ahead, looming up out of the mists and drifting snow, the summit of Francés, another unclimbed peak, and the approach looked easy. I filmed a lot during this part of our ascent and the shots I took then were some of the most beautiful I have ever taken in the mountains. For a while I unroped from the other three to film shots of them as minute specks in the huge arena of ice and snow and drifting mist, to show how puny and insignificant man is in this wild world.

Eventually we climbed into the blue shadow of the summit

and the temperature fell. The angle of the ice steepened and we zig-zagged our way up with a feeling of great exposure as we edged out across a sweeping slope that fell for 1,000 feet or more to the glacier below. A fall here would have been disastrous. After a while we struck the final ridge about fifty feet below the summit, climbing into the brilliant sun again. The top of Francés was made up of three enormous cauliflower mounds of ice crystals, each about thirty feet high. We kicked steps in these easily and at five o'clock the four of us stood on the summit of Monte Francés, height about 7,033 feet.

We had climbed up through the mists and to the west lay a thick sea of cloud stretching towards the Pacific. The higher peaks of the Darwin Range stuck out like fingers of ice and Eric was able to identify Darwin and Yahgan, the two peaks he had climbed last year, while beyond lay a jumble of unexplored and unknown mountains.

Below our feet the slopes of Francés plummeted to Puerto Olla where we had landed, and we could see Devil's Island lying at the divide of the Beagle Channel, bathed in warm sunlight and lapped by brilliant blue water. To the east we could see the Beagle Channel, a narrow cut-through past Navarino Island and the main island of Tierra del Fuego, stretching for 120 miles almost to the Atlantic.

We lingered for about one and a half hours, in spite of the cold, wondering at the beauty, and loath to leave our eyrie. Then as the great, pyramidal, indigo shadow of Francés began to edge out over the plateau, pointing towards where our tent was pitched, we realised we had a steep and difficult descent to make in only a few hours of daylight. Reluctantly we turned and started to belay each other down the sheer, smooth ice slopes. Peter had a small slip and I remember hearing my voice high and brittle with fear, shouting to tell him to take care, as if he was not already being as careful as he could. Talking with Eric years after, recalling this descent, I found that he also had sensed the danger of this icy slope and felt that this was one of the dangerous moments of his life. Ice-screws had yet to be invented. Crampons, ice-axe and rope were all we had.

Soon, however, the angle eased off and we strode quickly

Mount Darwin, at approximately 8,700 feet, the highest peak in the Darwin Range and first climbed by Eric Shipton in 1962, seen here from the summit of Monte Francés.

Peter Bruchhausen and Eric Shipton arrive at the Chilean navy lighthouse near Devil's Island to await collection.

The friendly Chilean navy vessel *Beagle* delivered us to Puerto Williams and en route we helped them load wool along the Beagle Channel.

and easily down into the deep, cold shadow on the glacier and a sky livid with pinks, mauves and duck-egg blue. As we approached the Pyramid tent, the colours reminded me of the paintings of Wilson of the Antarctic. Then we were there. If we had to live normally under the cramped conditions of that tent back in Britain, we would probably only stick it for a few days, but for us now, returning from the first ascent of Francés, it was our home, It represented warmth, food, security, even comfort. We crawled inside, contented, happy, men at peace with the world and each other. My diary says: "Good fug, gallons of tea and then a meal. Bed late. What a day!"

Almost as if resenting our success and keeping up its usual rhythm, the weather once again became ferocious. When we woke the sleet and blown drift were rattling on the tent, as violent gusts of wind howled across the glacier. For a while it looked as if it was going to improve, when thin sunshine oozed through the clouds, but in the end it closed in again and we stayed snugly in our bags. The sudden blasts of wind made the sleet and hard granules of snow drum on the tent like lead shot, while the canvas flapped and cracked. At times it was almost impossible to talk above the din and we lay and wondered if the sturdy Pyramid would stand up to yet another onslaught.

The blown snow began to pile up on our windward side and we could see the heavy bulge increasing and gradually forcing the tent wall down. Already the force of the wind had bent the strong poles on this side in an arc, and we felt that any more weight might snap them. Digging this snow away had been one of our major daily chores. On this day my diary noted that it was Claudio who went and did the unenviable task, but the bee in my bonnet about his not pulling his weight was still there and I rather unkindly wrote: "Claudio went out and dug about rather hysterically and then came in and soaked everything. It is really the first time he has done anything for the community. He even lit the Primus and cut up the meat bar." Poor Claudio. I like to think that I never showed this resentment I had for him. Sleep was difficult that night because of the rattle of sleet and the crack of canvas.

We carried a small altimeter, which of course served as a barometer. When we woke after a night of fitful sleep it showed that the pressure was very low. Outside it was comparatively calm except for the small flurries of snow. Eric felt we had carried out all the exploration we could do in this area and that Roncagli looked a difficult mountain to attempt from this side. So, as time was getting short and the weather pattern deteriorating, he decided it would be better now to get back to the Beagle Channel to wait for the Chilean navy to pick us up. It had been nearly three weeks since we had left Punta Arenas.

We packed what we could inside the tent, kneeling and pushing at the sleeping bags and clothing to get them stowed safely away; pummelling at our Li-los to deflate them and rolling them up so that the stale air came out in great gusts with little puffs of French chalk blown out on its breath. I never did this job without remembering the splendid story that Hugh Ruttledge (the leader of the 1933 Everest expedition) once told me, of how terrible the stench was when they deflated their Li-los on Everest after the Sherpas had been to a *chang* party the night before!

We then crawled out of the empty tent to find the wind was getting up. I suppose we ought to have realised what was in store for us by the low barometric pressure. We had a fearful struggle to free the tent. Our body heat and cooking had melted the snow under and around the ground sheet. The canvas itself was frozen stiff and the snow on the valance had turned to hard ice and had to be hacked away. The pegs were buried deeply in the frozen snow and also had to be cut free with our ice-axes. All the time we were doing this, the wind was getting stronger and we were working in white-out conditions, as the blown snow whirled about us.

After two and a half hours we were packed up and ready to go, already pretty wet with the powder snow driven up our sleeves and down our necks. As well as carrying our heavy rucksacks we decided to tow the three kit bags behind us in order to remove everything in one go, instead of relaying. The compass seemed to be playing weird tricks and, in thick mist and blown snow, we set off much too far to the east and found ourselves on steep ice, something we had not expected. Claudio, who was carrying the tent poles, somehow managed to drop them and we saw them disappearing down the steep slope into the mist. It could have been a disastrous accident, for we would have been deprived of our only means of warmth and shelter, but, miraculously, a sudden clearing blew across and revealed them lying near a crevasse a hundred yards away. We cramponed down to them and this time made sure Claudio had tied them firmly on to his rucksack.

We set off once again more by guess work than bearing, but luckily there were a few more clearings and we were able to see the edge of an outcrop of rock which we recognised and that gave us some idea of our position. The weather gradually became worse and worse and we were now fighting straight into the wind. I was in the lead at this stage, leaning and clawing my way forward. Three times I had the unnerving experience of breaking through the soft snow up to my waist, with my legs kicking over the green and blue icy depths of gaping crevasses. Icicles hung and clattered in Eric's beard and mine. We reached the edge of the outcrop of rock and the wind increased even more. It seemed impossible that it could, but it was now like a thing possessed, grabbing and buffeting at us. The air seemed to be almost solid and visible and it was as if we were straining into an endless barrage of rushing waves. We were all picked up and hurled twenty or thirty feet several times, which on steep ice is not a pleasant experience. After being bowled over like wrestlers taking a fall, we struck out with the picks of our ice-axes and lay panting and terrified, waiting for the blast to diminish slightly before struggling to our feet once again. On a few yards, and then we were grabbed and knocked over again. It was an exhausting progress and all the time we were dragging the heavy kit bags behind us as we went.

The route was heavily crevassed and in white-out conditions it was impossible to see the way. I came to one large crevasse and paused for a lull. I leapt across and half fell and floundered on the brink and finally furrowed my way to safety on the far side. Eric was carrying the tent, a huge, frozen, unmanageable load, weighing over eighty pounds, strapped to a pack-frame. He tried to leap the crevasse and failed. With horror, we watched him almost in slow motion, disappearing through the hole he had made. The rope tightened and as if in delight the wind enveloped us and shrieked with fury.

I crawled to the edge of the hole and saw Eric lying head down on a ledge or ramp about ten feet below. It was amazing luck he had landed on this, for he was perched above a frightening chasm into which, if he made an awkward move, he would fall. I had never heard Eric raise his voice at any time and he did not now. I just heard above the roaring of the wind his faint words. "Er, I say," he said, "are you going to be able to get me out?"

By hauling on the rope on my side of the crevasse and by Peter steadying him with his rope on the other, he was able to right himself and struggle out of the pack-frame, holding the tent that had been pinning him upside down on the edge of the drop. Making sure that Peter was safely anchored and holding Eric, I untied my rope and lowered the end down with two karabiners tied on to it. Eric was able to clip them on to the pack-frame, with the tent, and I was ready to try to haul the load up. The wind all the time had been plucking and hurling itself at us, and several times I was in great danger of being blown into the crevasse myself, as I heaved and strained at the awkward bundle of the tent, that kept getting wedged and stuck under the lip of the crevasse. It took a long time before finally it was landed, like a huge fish, on the surface of the glacier. The suspense, fear and cold had proved too much for Claudio and he sat and wept in the snow. Peter, pale and worried, kept muttering, "We shall all die", but in fact it did not take much longer for Eric to be extracted, like a tooth from a jaw, to join us in the whirling drift snow. The whole operation had taken some forty-five minutes.

It took some time to pull ourselves together and to reorganise the loads, during which time the storm continued in all its fury. By now I had no feeling in my hands and feet. I had had to take my gloves off to tie knots and lower the rope to Eric in the crevasse. Eric said that his toes were pretty numb too. It was no wonder for he, after all, had just spent forty-five minutes deep in the heart of the glacier. When we set out again the ice steepened and it was obvious we should have to put on our crampons. It was an appalling ordeal. The straps were frozen, our hands were numb and our fingers wooden. I remember fumbling and swearing and whimpering with rage, pain and frustration. At last, when we were all ready, on we went. By now I was shaking and shivering with cold. Drift snow had blown up and under our anoraks, down our necks, up our sleeves and we were soaked to the skin. The icicles on our beards were enormous. But at last we dropped below the cloud and snow flurries and crossed the last part of the glacier on to rock, even if it was rock covered in thick snow. We recognised where we were from our journey up many days before, and a sense of relief swept over me. We dumped the loads we had been sledging behind us and moved across to the long moraine ridge.

Poor Claudio, who was carrying the tent, was going very slowly and complaining about the weight, so I swapped over with him. I was rather afraid though that my rucksack weighed more! Halfway down the moraine ridge we found a ledge and were able to clear it for the tent. It was by then seven p.m. We had been fighting for our lives for nine hours. There had been moments when it looked as if we had lost, but the human animal has enormous resources of stamina which for most of our lives remain untapped. We had fought on with the will to live, that most important factor of all growing stronger every minute. And when it was over there was that deep, inner satisfaction and contentment, knowing that one had survived by one's own strength, skill and will-power.

We crept inside the dank tent and made the most marvellous cup of tea I have ever tasted, and then our supper of meat bar. My feet and hands began to thaw out with an agonising pain that made me bite my lips to prevent crying out. Both Peter and Claudio had very painful feet, too. The nail of one of Eric's big toes was black with frostbite and I was left with numb ends both to my fingers and toes for many months. We were lucky to escape with only these minor injuries. Deep, dreamless sleep soon took over as the storm still boomed around on the glaciers above, where we had so nearly perished.

Eric was surprisingly gloomy about the weather and reluctant to move. He thought that the snow was too deep for us to descend easily and that we should have to wade through up to our waists and that it would take a very long time to reach the Beagle Channel. However, by eleven we were ready to go and I led off, finding the going awkward but not too bad, as I worked across the steep moraine slopes, trying to reach the guanaco track. I must have been in a stupid "bash on regardless" frame of mind again for I got myself into difficulties on a steep rock and grass gully covered in soft powder snow, and with the eighty-pound tent on my back I was in every danger of peeling off. To make matters worse it started to snow heavily. Eric's premonitions looked like proving correct. He then traversed across to find another route and managed to get through to the guanaco track. I rather shame-facedly climbed down my gully and followed. But I had not really learnt my lesson and with youthful arrogance I was once again out in front, roaring ahead. It must have been infuriating for the others and I was really not being much help to them. If a group of four is moving across tricky ground with heavy loads, it should move together. The leader needs to pause just a little at each difficulty. I should have known better, for I had been with John Tyson in the Himalayas and had some ten Alpine seasons behind me and considered myself to be a competent and thoughtful mountaineer. I was to experience this sort of youthful arrogance from the other point of view in these mountains sixteen years later.

Being kind to our frost-nipped feet, we took three days to ferry all our gear down to the Beagle Channel. It was marvellous to be back at sea level with the sound of the gulls and the waves to replace the shriek of the wind and the crack of canvas. We sat by our fire, toasting and glowing on one side and cold on the other for it was still chill and winter was on the way. One thing spoilt it for me. My diary says: "No mussels here. Blast it!"

In the week that followed we had a chance to talk and unwind and leisure to explore this remote shore where no one had really lived since the days of the Yahgan and the Alacaluf Indians, whose tent-sites we identified by grassed-over mounds of mussel shells. There was time to stroll with Eric through magnolia and nothofagus trees, to talk to Peter about his work in the Antarctic, to watch kelp geese swimming completely unconcerned a few yards off, and to upset a whole sea-lion rookery when we motored across the Beagle Channel in our RFD.

From a distance it looked almost as if the rocks were rippling and moving, as the creatures shuffled about, but when we motored in closer to the shore we could see individual animals. There were many cows craning their heads towards us and here and there a huge bull with great, heavy fur-covered neck, branching whiskers and rheumy eyes. At first they were inquisitive but not frightened. I do not suppose that they had ever seen humans close to, though their ancestors would have been hunted by the Alacaluf and Yahgan. As we approached closer, the cows began to slither and slide off the rocks into the water. The bulls stood their ground longer. There was one grand old male, who watched us closely, refusing to be intimidated until the last moment, but after a few hesitant movements, he, too, leapt off the rocks into the sea with an enormous belly-flop. So ungainly and awkward on the land, these creatures were able to manoeuvre at great speed under the clear water of the Beagle Channel. They were not really frightened by us and every few seconds we were surrounded by bobbing heads, an amazing and hilarious sight. Rather cruelly, I suppose, we motored away for a while and we saw them laboriously clambering back on to the rocks. We gave them half an hour and then chugged back to watch, once again, their wild splashing dives into the water. The old bull, surrounded, like Henry VIII, by his six wives, was distinctly disgruntled, as one by one they deserted him, till he too, at last, reluctantly smashed into the water, sending out a minor tidal wave.

The sight of four scruffy, bearded people pottering about in a rubber dinghy in the remote waters of the Beagle Channel excited the curiosity of more than the sea-lions, and two Antarctic vessels of the Chilean navy stopped to investigate us. Claudio, who had final examinations to sit in Santiago, hitched a lift on one of them, but the rest of us were loath to return so abruptly to civilisation. We did, however, motor some ten miles east along the Channel to a remote manned lighthouse where we were able to have our arrival radioed to the Chilean navy.

My unremitting filming duties, which must have proved a sore trial to the others at times, now provided some congenial occupation in those last few days. I needed to film some cutaways, those sequences vital to the editing, and for once we were blessed with warm, idyllic weather and, as it turned out, beautiful sequences for the film. First we chugged westward in the dinghy towards the snout of the Italia Glacier, about five miles from Puerto Olla. On the way there we found another sea-lion rookery, which I filmed. Some of the sea lions swam with us into the bay which was full of small icebergs that had broken off the glacier. As we edged in through the floating ice, there was a deafening rumble and roar and we looked up to see a mass of ice break off the sheer wall of the glacier that plunged for over 1,000 feet into the Beagle Channel. This huge ice avalanche cascaded down the face and, with a thunder, crashed into the water, sending up a curtain of spray. A fairly large tidal wave surged across the bay towards the dinghy. We just had time to swing the bows round to face the onslaught. It was very obvious that we could not approach any closer to the face of the glacier without being either swamped or hit by falling blocks of ice, each the size of a house. Instead, we beached the boat and climbed to the top of some rocks about 200 yards from the icefall, and I waited with the camera. It proved remarkably difficult to film the ice avalanches, but after a few false starts, I managed to obtain what I hoped were some good sequences. As we motored away in the rubber dinghy the best fall of the day occurred. This sort of thing always seemed to happen when one had packed the camera away!

The other sequence I needed was to represent our climbing

up through the icefall on our first ascent of Bové. It had to be a cheat, but at least it was filmed on the Francés Glacier in the Darwin Range. I know of one climbing film of South America where the close-ups and cutaways were all filmed in a quarry back in Britain! We found a very beautiful section of crevasses and séracs about an hour from our camp and Peter and Eric clambered about, cutting steps, belaying each other and really doing some quite spectacular ice-climbing, that in fact was probably harder than what we had done on the actual ascent! It cut in to the film with no trouble and made a very lovely sequence with the deep blues and greens of the crevasses.

March 13th was to be our last day in camp. It was another glorious day and Eric and I had been out collecting bugs and beetles on the plain below the Francés Glacier and had now returned to the beach to gather mussels for another moules marinières. We were startled to hear shots in the distance and when we reached the point opposite Devil's Island there was a sudden loud bang and one of the Chilean naval lighthouse keepers appeared, with a gun over his shoulder and a dog at his heels. He had walked along the shore for eight miles, to tell us we had to go to the lighthouse with all our gear to wait for the Chilean naval ship that would arrive in two days to pick us up. We all wandered back to the camp and packed everything very quickly. In the rain we loaded the boat and with the lighthouse keeper, dog and all, pottered up the Beagle Channel past Devil's Island to the lighthouse.

Later on that day, when we had unloaded everything, Peter, one of the keepers and I took the empty dinghy out for a run. We had discovered that by pushing down on the wooden keel, getting the balance correct and opening the throttle on the motor, we could get the dinghy to plane. It rose up on top of the water, if it was calm, and skimmed along at high speed. It was most exhilarating and we roared about the bay. Suddenly we were aware that the sea was full of dolphins, flashing along with us, nearly bumping into the boat, rolling over and over in their excitement. A few even leapt into the air beside us and we saw intelligent eyes looking at us and the strange smiling mouths agape with fun, as if challenging us to race them.

We had mussels, followed by mussels and finally followed by mussels for our supper.

Now that we had definitely had the news that we would be picked up, there was a great reluctance to leave this fascinating area. Eric, Peter and I set off in the boat to the middle of the Beagle Channel so as to film and photograph Francés and Bové, towering high above the forests that fringed the shore. Francés, particularly, rose sheer from the water's edge in one continuous sweep from sandy shore and nothofagus trees to glacier, snow slopes and huge icy domes of frozen mist.

We had seen Devil's Island from the summit of Francés and now we decided to land and climb to its highest point. Eric told us that it had got its name from one of Fitzroy's men who, when he landed here, had been scared by an inquisitive owl and felt certain that he had come face to face with the devil when he saw the ghostly face and staring eyes. We saw neither an owl nor the devil, but we all wondered how many men had landed here since that first surveying party. It must have been very few.

The boat did not come that day and I think we were all secretly rather glad. We had obviously struck a period of fine, calm weather and I know I certainly had a sneaking regret that we were no longer up in the mountains, with the chance to explore further into the interior and possibly try an approach to Roncagli. It was so warm that I decided to have a swim in the Beagle Channel, mainly bravado, I suppose, but the thought of a bath was pleasant. The whole operation was made hazardous by the lighthouse keeper's gun dog which thought that I must be some form of huge duck to be retrieved, and splashed in after me and then chased me as I ran naked along the shore. Peter and Eric found this incident hilariously funny, as well they might!

The boat arrived at two fifteen, so we took all our gear and equipment over to it in the dinghy, while the crew landed provisions and coal for the lighthouse, and brought mail for the two men. The vessel was splendid. It was called the *Beagle* and was a wooden boat, about seventy feet long, and although it had a powerful engine, it had a mast and sails as well, a gaff cutter in fact. It was cold and windy when we set off and to supplement the engine the crew hauled up the mainsail and jib and we heeled over and creamed up the Beagle Channel. I suddenly became very much aware of the history of this incredible part of the world. Here we were sailing up the Beagle Channel in a boat called the *Beagle*. And I remembered that other Earle, the artist, who had sailed with Fitzroy and Darwin on the first *Beagle*.

The Chilean crew were great company. Suddenly they hoisted an additional flag; it was the skull and crossbones! As is so often the case with small units in the Services there is a great feeling of comradeship and *esprit de corps*. We sailed till late afternoon and then turned north into Bahia Yendegaia. We just reached the end of the bay and saw the ramshackle buildings of an estancia on the shore, as it grew dark. It was a calm evening and the water was glassy. A great black cliff rose on one side and beyond the estancia we could see a broad, flat, alluvial plain running north-west between sharp, rocky, triangular peaks to the Stoppani Glacier about ten miles away. The smell of grass floated out across the water. It was a remote and fascinating place and I knew that Eric, always with an eye for new and interesting places to explore, was already planning another expedition from here.

We rowed ashore and met Mr. Cerka, a huge shambling Yugoslav, the owner of the estancia. He made us most welcome and invited the captain of the *Beagle* and the three of us to have a drink, followed by a vast meal of mutton stew. Our shrivelled stomachs were so unused to large meals and our heads so unused to alcohol that, by the time we had had more drinks after the meal, I certainly felt both bloated and light-headed. In that state we were rowed back to the *Beagle* at midnight and snored on our Li-los in the captain's cabin.

The boat's diesels roared into life at five-fifteen a.m., which is more than can be said of us. It was, however, a most wonderful morning and the sunshine flooded the whole bay and the pointed peaks with an incredible mauve and pink light. The water was again absolutely still and seemed almost like an inverted sky, as we thudded our way due south across the

Beagle Channel to Hoste Island. We anchored just off the shore, where there was a small estancia, quite close to the historic Murray Narrows. Here we inflated our dinghy again and went ashore with the crew of the *Beagle*, who also brought their small rowing boat. They needed our help to load bales of wool on board to take to Puerto Williams; yet another example of the Chilean navy acting as a goods and passenger service in these remote regions. It speeded up the process enormously, to have our dinghy with its outboard engine, and it was good to feel we could be of some help.

After the work was done we called at the small building and were offered a glass of milk. Outside stood a remarkable old lady. The sailors told us that she was called Grandmother Chacon and was the last of the pure-blooded Yahgans. Eric and I were both intrigued to meet her and we talked of the famous Bridges family whom we were to meet in a few weeks. I asked her if I could take some photographs and she agreed, but said she would charge a small fee! As I later sold her photograph to the National Geographic Society for £40 it was a good investment and I wished I had given her more.

Our next wool-ferrying stint from an estancia at Puerto Navarino, just east of the Murray Narrows, disintegrated into hilarious chaos as an overloaded rowing boat sank under its burden and my last happy memory of our own little Voyage of the *Beagle* was sitting in the wheel house writing out the words of "What shall we do with a drunken sailor?" for the guitar-playing captain.

7

Pioneers and Indians

Back in Punta Arenas there was a distinct feeling that winter was on its way. Chill winds shrieked up the streets and the waves on the Magellan Straits were whipped into white caps. Eric and I were invited to a special cocktail party at the British Club for the officers of HMS *Protector*, on a courtesy visit after a summer Antarctic tour. I remember we both felt very scruffy as we had been back only a few hours and had straggling beards. Eric's toes were still painful and mine were still numb as were my fingers. We felt most ill at ease and half-throttled in our suits and unaccustomed collars and ties. It was a boozy affair, with, if I remember rightly, dancing, in which I did not participate!

Whenever I saw Eric in a suit I was reminded of the story he told of how he was invited to some important dinner after one of his expeditions. On this occasion he had not brought any smart clothes with him. The friends he was staying with insisted on lending him a dinner jacket, but Eric refused to wear the trousers, as he maintained that only his top half would be seen above the table. So he went to this important function wearing a white shirt, bow tie, dinner jacket coat – and jeans!

The next day we were invited on board HMS *Protector* to have the hair of the dog. Peter Bruchhausen had left us now and I was sorry to say goodbye. He had been a good companion and expedition man, with a great sense of humour and fun. I knew that it was unlikely that our paths would ever cross again.

Before we left Britain Eric had suggested I read the book, *The Uttermost Part of the Earth*, by Lucas Bridges. He said it was fascinating reading and would form a good background to my knowledge about Tierra del Fuego and the climbing. He also mentioned that after the expedition he planned to visit the Bridges family who lived on the eastern side of the island and he had written to them asking if I could join him. I had been able to borrow a copy of the book from the library of the Royal Geographical Society and for several days I had been completely absorbed. Not only was it a remarkable account of the history of the amazing pioneering Bridges family and how they came from Britain to settle in this bleak, wind-swept end of the world, but it was also a unique record of the Indians of Tierra del Fuego, the Yahgan, the Ona and the Alacaluf. The intimate and personal portraits of the people were so vivid, that I felt I myself had known both the Indians and the Bridges family personally, what they looked like, their characters and the lives they lived. It was therefore with eager anticipation that I joined Eric and his old friend Phyllis Wint, who had just arrived in Punta Arenas, at the airport for our flight south to Rio Grande on the eastern, Argentine coast of Tierra del Fuego. We were amused to see the emblem of the airline was a penguin, a bird that cannot fly. In spite of this possible handicap we flew uneventfully over the Magellan Straits and an hour later were being welcomed warmly by Oliver Bridges, a grandson of the original settlers.

Oliver first drove us into Rio Grande, a strange little settlement, with very much the feeling of a frontier town, like the set of a Hollywood wild west film. The main street was broad and many of the side roads unpaved. Very few of the houses were more than one storey high and many of them wooden or made of corrugated iron. A few had verandas opening on to the street.

We were soon out of the town and driving south along a dirt track with choking clouds of dust swirling up behind. The countryside was flat, brown and arid-looking. Away in the distance were low hills clothed in the dark green of the nothofagus trees. There was no bridge across the wide Rio Grande near the town, so we had to swing quite a few miles inland to where the river narrowed and a bridge was possible, then retrace our steps to the coast. After about forty-five minutes, we arrived at Viamonte, the estancia owned by the Bridges in this part of Tierra del Fuego.

I suppose I had carried in my mind some idea of what Viamonte would look like, after reading *The Uttermost Part of the Earth* and seeing the photographs there, but I had not anticipated the feeling of history, and the atmosphere of the place.

The low building, almost lost in the surrounding shrubs and flowers, was obviously big and T-shaped. We entered by a door in the centre of a large, bow-fronted veranda with windows all round it. Inside, was a huge wood-burning stove, standing four feet high. Everything was panelled in wood and there were several comfortable sofas and chairs as well as a great number of pot plants and flowers adorning the walls and tables. There was an air of great comfort and of an area that was used and lived in. This was the room where the members of the Bridges family who lived at Viamonte met, sat and talked during the summer months. For the cold winter months, there was a sitting room, further in the depths of the house, protected from the raw weather outside by a continuation of the glassed-in veranda, that ran as a passage along the whole length of the front of the main building.

Betsy, Oliver's American wife, was there to welcome us and show us to our rooms, large, comfortable and wood panelled. Later, Oliver introduced us to his brother Len. With their sister, Clarita, they are the grandchildren of Thomas and Mary Bridges, the original settlers in Tierra del Fuego, who came from Britain. Later, I met Aunty Bertha, as she was known to everyone. She was now eighty-four and one of the daughters of Thomas and Mary.

I had just experienced with Eric something of the difficulties and dangers of this harsh end of the world. Wandering along the shores of the Beagle Channel, perhaps more than anywhere else, I had felt strongly that I was an intruder into a strange, primeval world where man came, lived and survived only on sufferance. But the Fuegean wilderness presented an intensely exciting and fascinating challenge. I was intrigued to know why the Bridges family, especially Thomas and Mary, had succeeded in the face of appalling risks and hardship to settle here, and I began to realise that so much of it was the mental attitude; the same will to live that had saved us in the storm on Bové, in what is, without doubt, one of the most hostile environments of the world. The two expeditions with Eric into the untravelled wilderness had given me a chance to come to grips with the difficulties at a personal level, and to gain some insight into the problems that must have faced the early pioneers. By being with Eric I was able to see how this great explorer dealt with the hazards in very much the same way as Thomas and Mary must have done. He had visited and returned to these storm-lashed shores many times and was beginning to feel a sense of mastery of the environment, but never a feeling of complacency and familiarity, for that could become lethal within minutes.

It was with these feelings that I met and talked to the Bridges this time and resolved that, one day, I should come back to venture further into the wilderness of this haunting land, and research, with deeper insight than was possible on this short visit, the history of the family and how they faced up now to the new, different and complex challenges of the world today. Sixteen years later I was to have my wish.

Living as I did, and indeed still do, in Devon, I was extremely eager to visit one of the estancias owned by the Bridges family on the shores of the Beagle Channel, named Harberton after Mary Bridges' native Devon village. Both Oliver and Len were keen to do the journey to Harberton with

The cocktail hour at the British Club in Punta Arenas, straight off the boat and not at our sartorial best.

Life seemed one long binge at the hospitable Chilean airforce Met. Station at Puerto Eden on Wellington Island.

An Alacaluf Indian tent and dug-out canoe at Puerto Eden.

Below left: an Alacaluf woman selling mussels and miniature canoe souvenirs to visiting shipping at Puerto Eden. *Below right:* Grandmother Chacon, the last pure-blooded Yahgan Indian at Hoste Island in 1963.

me, for it was to be quite a milestone in the history of the Bridges family. It would be the first trip the family had made by land from Viamonte to Harberton, since the official opening of a new road.

Until this year no road, not even one that a Land-Rover or jeep could use, connected Harberton with the outside world. If one wanted to go there, a boat from Ushuaia or a horse from Lake Fagnano were the only means of travel. In the latter case one had to use an incredible track cut by Lucas Bridges with the help of Ona Indians, through the forests and swamps, over the mountains and unexplored country of the interior.

As we left Viamonte in the two Land-Rovers, Aunty Bertha came to see us off. Though eighty-four, her mind was as active as ever. "Make sure you have some matches with you," she called after us. "You never know when you might have to spend a night out in the open." She had had to do so many times as a young girl, and it was fascinating, later, to hear her talk about the early days of Harberton. Such remarks as, "I always had to carry the revolver. Alice did not like shooting," made me stare in astonishment at this little, frail, old lady who had been born and who had lived all her life in this wild country.

With the first golden tints of autumn splashing the countryside with colour, we set off on the main road from Rio Grande to Ushuaia. Beyond Lake Fagnano we climbed steeply up to the Garibaldi Pass and into the snow at a height of over 2,000 feet. Beyond, the muddy track to Harberton turned off the main road and we ground along in low gear, over the rough surface, through the forest. Six hours later we emerged from the forest on to the shores of the Beagle Channel and turned east towards Harberton. There was no track now and we followed the shore for a lot of the way. Once, one of the Land-Rovers broke through the treacherous surface of the swamp and we had to winch ourselves out. We ploughed across a tidal river and after twelve hours of a jolting journey we arrived at Harberton.

Tommy and Adrian Goodall, the great-grandsons of Thomas Bridges, welcomed us as did their mother, Oliver and

Len's sister, Clarita. The white, wooden and corrugated iron buildings stood beside the inlet, looking exactly as they must have done when they were built nearly eighty years before. Much of the wood in pre-fabricated sections, and the bricks for the foundations had come from Harberton in Devon and a lot of the building work had been done by two Devon carpenters, who had been with Mary and Thomas Bridges in those early days.

Life had not changed much since the family had first settled on this 50,000-acre farm. The weather was as rough and as raw as it always had been. In winter the days are short and the nights are long and bleak, for Harberton stands under the Southern Cross, only eighty miles from Cape Horn, and beyond, over Drake's Passage, lies Antarctica. They still kept vast flocks of sheep, 40,000 of them, that fed on pastures hacked out of forest and swamp. Supplies still came by boat from Ushuaia, but now, with the new track, more easily by road. Tommy Goodall also had a pilot's licence and he flew a light aircraft from a rough airstrip a few miles to the west of Harberton.

Len, Oliver and I walked up the hill beyond the farm, a place full of the atmosphere of adventure, bravery and enterprise. In the distance, below the jagged snow peaks, whales were spouting in the Beagle Channel. This was certainly a place to which I wanted fervently to return.

In Lucas Bridges' book mention is made several times of the Alacaluf Canoe Indians, who lived in the channels north of Tierra del Fuego, on the fiorded south-west coast of mainland Chile and who came south sometimes to attack the Yahgan and Ona. Eric, Jack Ewer and I on our journey to Mount Burney had travelled over some of the same lakes and fiords that the Alacaluf must have used, including, of course, the Passo del Indio. The Alacaluf spoke a different if similar-sounding language to the Yahgan and Ona, but very little was known about them, though they appear to have been an adventurous tribe, travelling great distances in their canoes, which, like those of the Yahgan, were made of bark, and were sometimes as long as twenty-nine feet. But they found that bark boats did not last for more than a few months and so they discovered the art of making dug-out canoes, which they propelled not only with paddles, but with oars in simple wooden rowlocks. They lived in small, dome-shaped huts made of leaves and skins, and ate shell-fish and hunted seals and birds with bows and arrows, spears and slings.

Before leaving Punta Arenas I wanted to see if I could make contact with this third tribe of Indians. I had been told that a few still lived at Puerto Eden, a third of the way between Punta Arenas and Puerto Montt, up the west coast of Chile. Puerto Eden lies on the east coast of Wellington Island. Puerto does not necessarily mean a port, but, as in this case, merely a place where it is possible to anchor in comparative shelter. The problem was to reach Puerto Eden. Although many ships thread their way through the maze of islands and the labyrinth of narrow channels of this fantastic coastline, very few of them stop there. Luckily, however, the *Navarino*, a Chilean passenger ship, was due to sail from Punta Arenas and they agreed to put me ashore there. I should hasten to explain that I was not, as it were, being "thrown" to the Indians, for the Chilean air force had a manned meteorological station nearby.

I had quite a number of days to spend in Punta Arenas as the exact sailing date for the *Navarino* was splendidly uncertain. It seemed as if they were waiting to make sure they had enough passengers and cargo to make the voyage worthwhile. One person I met passing through Punta Arenas while I was waiting was Chris Bonington who had just returned from the Towers of Paine, having successfully climbed the Central Tower. He was just setting off with his wife on a wandering return to Britain up the west coast of Chile. The Whillans Box Tent had evolved on this expedition, but this time Chris had no tent to use for his holiday! He therefore borrowed the sturdy Meade I had used on Mount Burney.

On April 21st we had word that the *Navarino* was likely to sail that day, so at one p.m. Bert Sheriff, the endlessly hospitable headmaster of the British School, collected me and my gear, which included the RFD dinghy and outboard engine, and drove to the docks. I had to pass through the Customs, as Punta Arenas is a free port, but soon we were on the quay and gradually the crowds began to collect with a strange, expectant excitement. Eventually all my baggage was stowed on board and I found my four-berth cabin. The *Navarino* was rather like the ships that ply between the Outer Hebrides.

As far as we could tell she was not going to depart at once; nobody really knew, except to say that, when everything was ready, we would go! After tea with Bert at the school, he drove me yet again to the docks and found the crowds even greater, milling about like spectators at a football match. Many were now clambering on board with packages of all shapes and sizes and also mattresses, which they dumped down in the open hold in the rain and cold. They were apparently going to travel there, for they had gathered in little family groups with all their food, bundles and screaming children.

Now winter was approaching, a lot of the seasonal work on the estancias, such as shearing and dipping, was over. Work in the freezers was finishing also, and these were workers from the Island of Chiloe and the mainland near Puerto Montt, who trekked south for the summer and returned home for the winter. Their ambition was to make as much money as possible over the years, then buy a smallholding in Chiloe and settle there. This island and the nearby mainland is a delightful part of Chile with a kinder climate than that of Tierra del Fuego. There are many little islands with neat fields and small farms on the fiorded coastline, while inland tower great, snow-covered, conical volcanic peaks.

About five p.m. we sailed, setting off down the Magellan Straits and, after a few hours, swung into the north-west arm of the Magellan Straits, through Paso Froward and the Paso Ingles. Now that the voyage had really begun, I had time to make contact with my fellow passengers. At supper, I sat next to a tall, bearded American, wearing a poncho. I discovered he was also one of the other three in my cabin. Like many Americans, in my view, he talked too much, but he was an amusing companion. We had some good Chilean wine for supper and afterwards, in the lounge, the American and I were joined by a Greek-German-Chilean who spoke excellent English. So many Chileans are a mixture of European races.

Suddenly I was greeted by a broad Liverpool accent and two scruffy characters sidled up. They introduced themselves as Rob and Brian, two PE teachers doing a round-the-world trip by hitching, working on cargo boats (which was possible without a union ticket back in 1963), and getting odd jobs here and there to boost their funds. They were travelling down in the hold with the seething mass of Chilean families and they asked if I could look after some records and a camera for them in the comparative safety of the cabin. They were both tough and amusing characters. We chatted until late evening about climbing, but had the sad experience of the steward refusing to serve Rob and Brian with any drinks because they were travelling third class and should not have been in the saloon.

The voyage took on a strange, dreamlike quality with eccentric, unexpected people flitting in and out of the various sequences. The American leapt out of his bunk at seven-thirty to take a shower, but I continued to doze till I felt it was a civilised time for breakfast. I had been spoilt for sea travel by my voyage to and from India, by P and O, on an expedition to Kanjiroba eighteen months before – a most civilised, cheap and splendid way to travel, sadly no longer possible in our jet-minded age.

At one thirty, we passed into the Smyth Channel that we had seen from Mount Burney and in vain I looked for the mountain. Unhappily, low cloud hung over the peak, but I could just see some of the glaciers radiating like spokes of a wheel from the hub of the summit. It seemed so remote and distant, it was hard to believe that we had struggled our way round the mountain in appalling weather only three months before.

I needed to make definite arrangements to be picked up when the *Navarino* returned from Puerto Montt to Punta Arenas. I did not relish the idea of spending the winter with the Alacaluf. The sailing date from Punta Arenas had been so vague, that I could not believe that I should even manage to find out when they were likely to return, but after a long talk with the first mate and the chief steward and with the help of the Greek-German-Chilean, they told me that, in about three weeks, they most certainly would collect me. We used the cabin as a meeting place and at first the Greek-German-Chilean came and talked and drank beer.

Rob and Brian came next and talked and wrote letters. The hold was apparently great fun if you were Chilean and knew everyone. Next a Catholic priest wandered in and talked about cameras. After supper, we bought some bottles of wine and about ten people gathered in the cabin to talk. Halfway through the evening the American left to take a shower! In fact I did not blame him, for the heat was intense and what with the wine, I had a splitting headache before everyone eventually left and I could get to bed. At one forty-five a.m., I was woken, running with sweat, by tremendous bangs and judders as the anchor went overboard. I felt as if someone had screwed a metal band round my head and then tightened it. The inside of my mouth was like old tripe. In my dazed state of mind, I thought we were already at Puerto Eden, which of course we were not, as I discovered by tottering out on deck in the dark and rain. Sweating sleep, full of fearful dreams, followed until the American went off for a shower at seven thirty.

I had been told that we would probably arrive between eight and ten, but it was not until eleven thirty that we came through the narrows and there was Puerto Eden behind several islands. The mountains were wreathed in low mist and a heavy drizzle swept across the bay as the *Navarino* dropped anchor. Suddenly from all directions small boats paddled out from the islands and from the shores of Wellington Island itself, and within two minutes the Alacaluf had swarmed aboard.

Their features were in many ways like the Nepalese. They had black, straight hair, brown skins, high cheek bones and almond-shaped eyes. Nearly all of them had magnificent white teeth, presumably because of the enormous intake of vitamins in their diet of seafood and seaweed. Where they originated from is not really clear, but Polynesia has often been suggested as one source. The other suggestion was that, like many of the

Indians of the Americas, they came from Asia across the Bering Straits to what is now Alaska and over thousands of years have spread down the whole length of the continent.

For their model bark canoes and the little baskets of plaited reeds which they brought to sell, they asked a thousand pesos, about twenty-five pence. They also had mussels and cholgas, an enormous type of mussel, for sale, but some cigarettes, an old shirt, food or some apples for barter seemed to suit them just as well as money. They spoke a little Spanish when doing their bartering, but among themselves, they still used their own language; strange guttural throaty sounds, with many hard syllables and clicks, similar to the Aboriginals of Australia and the Kalahari Bushmen and the Eskimos. Later I was to make some tape recordings of their speech, which I found fascinating.

I was taken ashore with all my gear, the RFD and the outboard, by the three FACH men from the Chilean air force meteorological station after their launch had finished loading a great many sacks of mussels for Puerto Montt aboard the *Navarino*. Several of the welcoming boats had heavy old bronze diving helmets and other compression gear in them. There was one other passenger, an enormously fat person who turned out to be the German-Chilean owner of a small canning factory on the far side of the channel. A concrete path led from the jetty to the comfortable wooden building that was the meteorological station, while strung out along the shore, just above high water mark, was the Alacaluf village. There were two wigwam-like huts, dome-shaped and made of seal skins, reeds, grass, driftwood, old pieces of canvas and iron sheeting on a framework of wood. Three other huts were made of wood and corrugated iron, but a seal skin still covered the roof of one. The two wigwams had no chimneys and smoke poured out of the roof through the reeds. In these five dwellings lived fifty-one Alacaluf – eighteen men, twelve women, twenty children and a vast number of mangy dogs.

Apparently back in 1953 there had been one hundred of these Indians and in ten years their numbers had dropped to half. Several reasons had been put forward, but it was generally accepted that now that they wore clothes, they no longer had the natural, physical resistance to the cold, raw climate of the Chilean channels. Also during their contact with white people, they had picked up diseases, such as measles, which proved fatal to primitive tribes the world over. But thanks to the Chilean air force sending food and supplies the death rate has decreased and the Alacaluf are now likely to remain a healthy and active tribe. The three FACH men did much to help the Indians and treated them with kindness and understanding, one of them with medical training holding daily surgeries.

I was interested to find three dug-out canoes still in use, but the boats they make are now clinker built and I was astonished to see the skill used in their construction. All the wood had to be cut and shaped into planks with only an axe and then fitted on to the framework. The joins, naturally, were not perfect and they caulked the cracks with strips of cloth, reeds or slithers of wood. The rowlocks and oars they also shaped with an axe from slender branches or tree trunks.

Later that afternoon, a tanker arrived in the bay and hooted as its anchor rumbled down. The Alacaluf shot out from the shore in their boats, as indeed did the air force men. Even though I had been here a few hours, I also caught the excitement that a passing ship caused; a contact with the outside world, other people with whom to talk. It was a Panamanian iron-ore carrier under an Argentine flag. The captain welcomed us on board and was intrigued to meet me, an Englishman, staying in this unlikely and forlorn place. He plied us with whisky and then insisted on giving me a bottle of whisky and a jar of jam. We zig-zagged our way back to the shore in fine form.

Supper that night was the first of the incredible shellfish gastronomic delights that the station sergeant prepared. It consisted of various types of clams, sea urchins, mussels and cholgas.

Shellfish are also the Alacalufs' staple diet. They appeared to have three methods of collecting them. No longer do the women have to dive into the depths of the icy waters to bring them to the surface. Instead, I watched two men, Utechakisto and Ockcheera, hauling up the great streamers of kelp that fringed the shores with large clusters of mussels in their roots. Another method was to use a long-handled rake to scrape the shellfish off the rocks or the bottom of the seashore and pull them to the surface. I saw Pathagen and Kalamack doing this one day at the mouth of the river, searching for small clams. The last method was to use a long pole, the end of which had been split open to pick the mussels and sea urchins off the rocks. I spent three hours with Wuksadia, who was over seventy, as she did this on a calm, sunny day, from her dug-out canoe, with the snow on the mountains reflecting on the glassy water behind her. Although the Alacaluf use a net for fishing, this is not the usual way for them, as nets are too costly and there are no natural materials from which they can make them. The one I saw them using had been lent by the owner of the mussel-canning plant a few miles up the channel from Puerto Eden. I gathered that the old method the Alacaluf used to employ was a simple rod and a line.

There are exciting tales told of how in the past the Indians used to creep up on sea-lions and club them to death, or catch the numerous cormorants and kill them by biting their necks. This no longer happens. Each of the eight Alacaluf families now had a gun. The only other food I saw them collecting were the wild berries called mortilla, that grow in autumn on the hills behind their village. These they either ate raw or boiled in water. They grow no crops, indeed the weather is so cold and the ground so wet that very few crops will grow here. Instead, though, I saw them begging for wheat from one of the ships that anchored nearby during my stay.

On the day after my arrival, yet another tanker anchored at Puerto Eden, this time Chilean. Once again we all roared out to it and as by this time I had the RFD inflated we arrived even quicker. As was always the custom, it appeared, we were invited on board, and within minutes the drinks were handed round. I suddenly had the feeling that my stay on Wellington Island was turning into one perpetual booze-up. Only a few hours seemed to pass without a drink. The third day at Puerto Eden was to prove the most alcoholic of my stay. It was a marvellous, calm morning with wreaths of mist lying over the water and the smoke rising up straight from the Alacaluf huts. The sergeant at the station told me that a tanker was due to arrive in half an hour and we would be throwing a party. We got the RFD ready and as soon as the ship glided into the bay, the long ripples surging like huge sea serpents across the glassy water, we roared out to it. Not far behind, paddled the Alacaluf to sell their model canoes and mussels. We were invited on board (as always) and I was delighted to find the chief engineer spoke very good English. Although it was only ten a.m., wine and cake were produced, which we tackled in the chief engineer's cabin. The sergeant then needed to return to the land to prepare the feast, so I took him ashore and later returned to fetch the captain, the pilot and chief engineer and another officer from the tanker, which was called the *Isabella*.

The meteorological station had been transformed for the party; everything was neat and tidy. The table was laid, with paper napkins and, down the centre, lighted candles. I never found out why this particular day was celebrated, but celebrated it certainly was. Another staggering seafood meal was prepared, starting with an "Assiette de Fruits de Mer", of which the best Brittany restaurant would have been proud. It was followed by mussels and cholgas cooked in various ways with interesting sauces. The sergeant, whose Christian name turned out to be Diogenes, obviously used the long hours when he had no duties to perform with the weather observations, concocting new and superb recipes. His enforced stint as a hermit in the "tub" of Puerto Eden had its recompenses after all. Martini, wine and then whisky flowed, many toasts were offered and everyone became merrier and merrier. Diogenes, having prepared the meal, did not, in fact, eat anything, so when we eventually set off to return the captain and his officers to the tanker, he had the greatest difficulty in reaching the jetty and getting up the gangway of the *Isabella*. Once on board, more drinks were produced and so it went on. The fat German from the canning factory was also there, so more toasts were proposed and drunk before we finally left.

Diogenes had now to negotiate the gangway again, down to

the dinghy. It became one of those classic drunk jokes. As he reached the last few steps of the gangway, I could see him focus with difficulty on the RFD, concentrating so much that his mouth hung open and his brow was furrowed. He paused, gathered all his reeling balance and launched himself towards the dinghy. One of the criteria of good jokes is that you should let your audience know what is going to happen just a few seconds before it does. This instance was no exception. We watched almost mesmerised, as Diogenes, with his eyes still firmly fixed on the dinghy, walked in a steady and dignified way, without even staggering, straight into the sea; he missed the dinghy by three feet at least! We laughed until it hurt and tears ran down our cheeks. Again in classic fashion, his hat went floating away and for a moment there was no sign of him. When he reappeared we fished him out and unbelievably, on the way back to the shore, dripping wet, he went to sleep, to be helped to his bed, and presumably dry clothes, by his two companions, when we had safely arrived. It had been quite a party!

The Alacaluf had also been given a large quantity of wine and they were already very drunk. Most of them were sitting in one of their larger huts, moaning and crooning. It was a sobering thought for a so-called civilised man for me to realise that we had killed them off in their hundreds through debilitation and disease, and finally taught them the bad habits of our own world, and listening to their drunken howls, I felt not a little ashamed.

The FACH men were thrilled to have a fast, mobile means of transport at their disposal and on many of my filming trips they came along to get to know, it appeared for the first time, the many islands, inlets and bays of this area. There were a surprising number of settlements in the channels, other than those of the Alacaluf, one of which was the canning factory owned by the German-Chilean. On several occasions the air force men, especially Diogenes, wanted to pay a special call on the owner. Perhaps factory is a word that gives the wrong impression of the dilapidated wooden huts scattered along the beach. However, here in this empty corner of the world a surprisingly busy industry had sprung up. The fat German-Chilean employed a number of men, including some of the Alacaluf, on a temporary basis to collect the cholgas. Several of the Chilean workers were divers, using the old "hard hat" diving suits and working at depths of between thirty and eighty feet in the clear but icy water. Many had the strange, slightly puffy features of professional divers.

Two processes were carried out in the factory. One was to string the five- to six-inch-long cholgas on cord and smoke them over a wood fire. They were delicious and I brought some strings home with me eventually, not, I hasten to add, in my personal luggage by air, but with the rest of the gear by boat. They survived the journey and were eaten with delight back in Britain, but it was some time before the smell of smoked cholgas got out of my tent and sleeping bag. The other process was a simple canning plant, powered by a small generator which produced hundreds of tins of cholgas in brine every year to be sold all over Chile. I have a feeling that the building and the whole set-up would not pass any British health inspector's scrutiny, nor the factory safety regulations, but the product was tasty and certainly did not poison me. The friendly owner gave me several tins to take home.

On the way back from this visit, as always, full of Argentine whisky, we intercepted some Alacaluf out collecting firewood. This was a great problem for them, as they had no firewood collecting policy, such as the Sherpas have, and were being forced further and further afield in their canoes, to find wood near the shore to load and bring back. They use a vast amount of wood, for they try to keep their fires going night and day.

While the Alacaluf were most friendly to me, it was incredibly difficult to make any real contact with them, mainly because my Spanish was so poor, and that was the only way I might have found out more about them. I was invited only once into a wigwam with the FACH medical corporal, because one of the very young children was unconscious. We later discovered it had been given a lot of wine to quench its thirst – no wonder the poor mite was insensible. The interiors of their huts and wigwams were dark and smoky. Indeed, one of the memories I still hold of the Alacaluf is the strong smell of smoke that pervades all their clothing and hair. Inside, they kept a few pots and pans near the fire in the centre of the floor and at one end there were bundles of reeds and leaves and skins that they used for beds. Their few belongings they kept in bundles, either hanging from walls or stacked in the corner.

On the whole I found them an unhappy, forlorn and in-bred people with no music, art or primitive culture of their own and with nothing gleaned from or given by the rest of humanity. Some of them had radios, but the broadcasts were mainly meaningless because of their lack of Spanish and understanding about the outside world. They were in that most difficult state of all primitive people, halfway between simple, nomadic life and modern civilisation. They were not sure to which world they belonged and if they thought about the future at all, which I doubt, then it must have seemed hopeless and meaningless. As it was, life for the Alacaluf must have been totally governed by the needs of the immediate future. If there was enough food, firewood and clothing, or some additional supplies to be begged or bartered from a passing ship, some wine to drown their sorrows perhaps, then life was, I suppose, acceptable.

My dinghy caused much delight and often laughter. Several times I towed their canoes behind me to the mussel-collecting grounds, with the blunt wooden bows pushing up a huge wave, as the boat shot through the water, far faster than it had ever been before or indeed was designed to go. Yercorekso hung on to his steering oar and roared with laughter as we covered the five miles beyond the islands in half an hour. The great journeys down the channels among the islands, even as far as Seno Skyring, across which we had forged on our trip to Mount Burney, were usually no longer made. But while I was there, one group of three, accompanied by at least eight dogs, went for a five-day trip collecting cholgas and while away on such a voyage, they lived in wigwams that had been constructed at strategic points. On my own journeys in the area in the rubber dinghy, I came across several of these dwellings, dome-shaped and made of bent sticks lashed with creepers, and covered with leafy branches and reeds.

While the group were away, I often thought of them, huddled at night over their fire, eating mussels on some lonely island, for this was the true life of the Alacaluf. At their backs, the thick, damp forest stretched up the steep mountain to the snows and glaciers, and at the door of their simple hut, were the stormy, icy waters of the channels. Their voyage back to Puerto Eden would not be easy, for a knife-sharp north-westerly wind was whipping the channels up into fierce, driving waves as the bleak dawn put an eye over the edge of the snowy peaks.

Three weeks passed very quickly, until the morning Diogenes told me that he had heard on the radio that the *Navarino* was close and I ought to prepare my gear for the return to Punta Arenas. The *Navarino* hooted twice. The Alacaluf paddled out and I was soon aboard. With farewells and promises to write, I thanked the three Chilean air force men for their kindness and for looking after me so well. The Alacaluf watched impassively as I waved, and we were gone. Puerto Eden slipped behind the wooded island, the drizzle closed in and that episode of my life was gone for ever, leaving very mixed, partly unhappy, memories of the Alacaluf.

I now wanted to get home as fast as I could. After nearly five months of wandering, I needed to get back to my own people, my own environment and my own language. There comes a stage on all expeditions when one has had enough and all one wants to do is to go home, and I had now reached that stage. Though not one of the most beautiful parts of Britain, London Airport on a bright May morning looked and smelt good.

The people of Britain were recovering from one of the worst winters in living memory. "I am just back from an expedition," I told my friends.

"Oh, missed the winter here, did you?" they said. "You were pretty lucky. It was terrible. The snow was here for months. Couldn't get the car out for weeks. All the water pipes burst. Didn't have water for a fortnight. Oh, you were very lucky to miss it."

I kept very quiet. No one really wanted to hear about my frozen toes and fingers or the blizzards in the Darwin Range.

8

Eric

Over the years that followed, Eric Shipton and I used to meet quite often and our friendship strengthened and matured. We talked a lot about expeditions and people. He always wanted me to return with him to South America, but sadly, having got myself involved in the sort of world on which he had been able to turn his back, it was never possible. I had made a niche for myself in television films, as a cameraman/director and while I continued to go on expeditions, I always had to persuade the television producers to let me make films in order to make a living. "Shipton and South America" had already been done, as far as they were concerned, and that was that. I could not make more films on the same subject. I always admired, perhaps slightly enviously, the singleness of purpose that Eric brought to exploration. He had made the decision on how his life was to progress and carried it out, not selfishly but, with complete and utter devotion and determination.

When we met, I often used to complain about being tied to the BBC's apron strings, especially as I became a presenter for quite a number of years, of a children's programme called "Tom Tom", which made it impossible for me to travel on large, long expeditions. As might be expected many of the items I presented on "Tom Tom" were to do with mountains and mountaineering. I persuaded Eric to appear once with me to talk about the pre-war Everest expeditions and also our two South American trips together. For the part of the programme dealing with Everest, we had had the unprecedented good luck of being able to borrow, from the Alpine Club, the treasured ice-axe that had belonged to Mallory. It had been found by Wyn Harris just above Camp VI on Eric's first Everest expedition in 1933. It was, of course, Eric's good name that had made this loan possible. After the programme Eric had offered to take the ice-axe back to the Alpine Club, as he was returning to London from the BBC television studios in Bristol.

Months later with that splendid half amused and half shame-faced look he had when telling stories against himself, which he often did, Eric confessed what had happened on his return to London. His car had been very full with luggage and plants that he and Phyllis Wint had bought. When they reached their basement flat in Tite Street, unloading had been an awkward task carrying things down the steps in several relays. Mallory's ice-axe had been put down on the pavement beside the car to be fetched later. Somehow, once in the flat, Eric had become distracted by something and both he and Phyllis had completely forgotten the axe. Hours later with an appalling jolt Eric remembered it and had shot up the steps to find, of course, that it had disappeared completely. Recounting the story Eric's eyes twinkled as he described how through a sleepless night he had prepared in his mind lengthy speeches for the Alpine Club Committee on how the famous Mallory ice-axe had been left lying in the street.

The next morning, however, there was a ring at a bell and on the doorstep stood a policeman, clutching the Mallory ice-axe. With a knowledge of his beat one would expect more of a village bobby than his London cousin, he considerately explained, "Knowing you to be a climbing gentleman, I guessed that this was some form of climbing implement. But I found it too late last night to return it to you then." So the Mallory ice-axe was returned safely to the Alpine Club, where it remains to this day. I doubt if it will ever be allowed to leave 74 South Audley Street again, but it certainly provided Eric with a classic story against himself.

Whenever I periodically grumbled to Eric about being tied to television schedules, he would console me by pointing out how lucky I was to be able to travel at all, which in retrospect, of course, I was. I ballooned over the Alps and Britain, I travelled in Europe filming fire walkers, volcanoes and ice-axe makers amongst other things; I visited Canada, and when I finally shook clear of the children's programme, bigger expeditions followed to the Sahara, Baffin Island and the Himalayas again. What Eric did not realise, perhaps, was that I was sad that all this prevented my going with *him*, for every year he returned to Patagonia, Tierra Del Fuego and the Galapagos Islands, with one sortie to Alaska.

I remember meeting him in London just before he left for Alaska. Eric needed to get some equipment and he had with him the very thorough and lengthy list sent to him by the Americans who were organising the expedition. "Ten Vests. Twenty pairs of socks. Five pairs of quilted underpants," and so on. For a man who took just the clothes he climbed in and one pair of extra socks, I think he genuinely found the list almost beyond his ken.

"Quilted underpants?" he said to me. "I shan't really need those shall I? Do you know, I don't think I have ever been anywhere that is really cold!" 27,700 feet on Everest can hardly be called warm and this is the height that Eric had reached in the pre-war years. So he left the well-known equipment shop without the quilted underpants, carrying his one pair of extra socks and what is called, I believe, a bambino rucksack!

When he visited me, he hated to do nothing and I remember his digging our vegetable garden on Dartmoor. We walked and jogged on the moors and once we traversed round the end of Berry Head near Brixham on a stormy day.

When we met in London, we would talk about his latest expedition and we would go into the Royal Geographical Society to look at maps and plan future trips, both real ones, and "wishful thinking" ones that might never happen. Time and time again he mentioned Yendegaia and how he would like to try an approach into the Darwin Range that way, a sort of back door to get to those glaciers we had seen to the north of Bové, including, of course, the great Stoppani Glacier.

In Shropshire we would walk and visit friends, and he would work in his vegetable garden. Eric had developed a love of and fascination with growing vegetables and delighted in the hard physical work and then seeing the produce flourishing. I do not think that I ever repaid all the hard work he had done in our garden, but I mowed his lawn once!

The last expedition (if it can be called such), when I travelled for some time with him, was the first Cook's tour to the Everest Base Camp in 1969, where he had been invited to be the leader and guest lecturer – yet another career starting. I was in Khumbu for three months, making a film about the Sherpas and I enjoyed being with Eric again for short spells amongst those great mountains, more than I can say. I still see the image of Eric looking very bronzed and fit, striding easily along with his marvellous, rhythmical pace to look up his old Sherpa friend Angtharkay. For Eric it was, of course, the first time he had been back to Everest, since his brilliant reconnaissance in 1951, when he was the leader of the small expedition that found the great Khumbu Icefall, the Western Cwm, and paved the way for the succesesful expedition to climb Everest in 1953.

This new career of leading tourist expeditions and lecturing on tour ships, puzzled many people who could not understand why this man, who loved solitude and the lonely parts of the world and, on the whole, shunned large crowds of people was, in their opinion, able to demean himself. But for Eric, it was just another means of travelling and he always took advantage of a journey to pack in some interesting trips of his own. He never stopped, always travelling, always finding out, always delighting in new places and old places re-visited.

In late 1975 when I had not seen Eric for several months I wrote one of my cheery letters asking how he was and what he had been up to, suggesting that we meet and have a talk. I had recently been in Baffin Island and I wanted to tell him about this trip. I had a sad, worried reply from Phyllis Wint who told me that she and Eric had been in Bhutan, with Eric acting as the guide for a group of Americans, and he had returned feeling very ill. For a while he thought it was some bug he had picked up out there and with sheer determination he would not give in, but at last, at the point of collapse, he was admitted to hospital. Cancer of the prostate and of the liver was diagnosed. He remained there for five weeks, and had many operations and was filled with drugs. The doctors talked about a chance of recovery, partly, one feels, for Phyllis and Eric's sake.

Early in 1976 I went to see him at Tite Street, on his release from hospital. I was dreadfully shocked by his appearance. He never carried any excess weight at any time, so now having lost a lot he was gaunt and haggard. But his spirit was indomitable. He either would not admit that he was not going to get better or he genuinely believed he was improving, but he had not given up. He was suffering enormous frustration at not being able to write, for he was in the middle of shortening *The Uttermost Part of the Earth* and writing about his long friendship with the Bridges family and his expeditions in Tierra del Fuego. He was also champing to get back to his garden in Shropshire. Spring was on its way and he knew there was a lot to be done.

He insisted that we went for a walk, though he ruefully told me that his pace was not what it used to be. We walked down Tite Street to the Thames. It was a cool February day and the gaunt black arms of the trees clawed at the foggy London sky. He walked very slowly. He was in no pain, but he felt very weak and as we walked, we talked. We turned up past the old herb garden of the Apothecaries and at once his active, searching mind released the mass of information stored there. He was, as always, enchanted by the world around him. I had to return to Devon that night. "I'll come and see you again after Easter," I said, "when you are better."

"Goodbye'" he said and we shook hands. Phyllis told me later that Eric had been deeply touched that I had travelled from Devon to see him.

Nicky Shipton, Eric's eldest son rang me in late March. "You will have heard about my Father," he said. "He died in Wiltshire a few days ago." I had not heard and I was completely stunned. Both Phyllis and he had been so confident that there was a good chance of recovery. I walked out into the night full of the misty scent of Dartmoor, with that deep, hollow despair and grief welling up inside me that only the death of some person very close can bring. I had not really known how close to Eric I had been and how fond of him I was until now. I walked for a while in the night until I felt that I could face people again, but the sadness remained and will remain for ever.

And yet one should not be sad. He had lived a remarkable and full life. He had been one of the great explorers and mountaineers of all time and had carried out so much of what he wanted to do and what he believed in. His sense of wonder and, as he puts it, "enchantment" never left him. The last paragraph of his autobiography sums it all up in that quiet, direct, unassuming prose that was the unique quality of his writing and the man.

> The springs of enchantment lie within ourselves; they arise from our sense of wonder, that most precious of gifts, the birthright of every child. Lose it and life becomes flat and colourless; keep it and

> "All experience is an arch wherethro'
> Gleams that untravell'd World, whose margin fades
> For ever and for ever when I move."

The springs of enchantment were still very much inside me, but as always, I had the worry of making my expeditions a way of making a living as well; films had to be made, photographs sold, articles or even books written. Since my first expeditions with Eric I had married and now had two sons and a wife to love and cherish. In recent years I had founded and was developing an Outdoor Pursuits Centre based on my Dartmoor farm and this also demanded my time and money to expand and run, in a period of spiralling inflation. It was Phyllis Wint, Eric's closest friend, who had really sowed the seeds of thought about my returning to Tierra del Fuego. We had naturally kept in touch since Eric's death and she had been talking about the shortened edition of *The Uttermost Part of the Earth* that Eric had been writing. The memories of my first visit to Viamonte and Harberton flooded back and I remembered my vow to return one day to make a longer film about the Bridges family at Harberton. With the incentive and the impetus there, the next stage of reasoning was obvious. I had always wanted also to return to the Darwin Range and I remembered how Eric had talked so much about starting an expedition at Yendegaia and pushing into the mountains from that direction, to the glaciers that he and I had looked down on from the summit of Bové. He used to use this proposed expedition as a "carrot" to get me to go back with him to South America – as if I needed a carrot. So, although it may sound emotional or glib, this new expedition of mine was to be partly a tribute to Eric and was certainly inspired by him and was to continue in a small way, his exploration of the Fuegean wilderness.

Two

1979

9

New year at gun point

In May 1978 various plans had fallen into place. I had Oliver
Bridges' blessing and my old friend Tom Salmon, station
manager of BBC Plymouth had accepted the proposal of a
film for Area Television about the link between Harberton,
Tierra del Fuego and Harberton near Totnes, with something
of the past history and present-day life of the Bridges family.
That I should write a book also looked a distinct possibility.
But one thing I did not want to happen was that people
should think I was climbing on to a band wagon and was
attempting to finish a book that Eric had started about the
Bridges; cashing in on Eric's death as it were. Some branches
of the Bridges family had been hesitant even about Eric's
attempting to abridge *The Uttermost Part of the Earth*, for
Lucas Bridges had expressly forbidden it in his will. The fact
that consent was eventually given for Eric to incorporate a
condensation into the framework of his own book was a
mark of conspicuous Bridges family esteem, and it was
something of a relief therefore when word finally came
through to me from David Bridges, Oliver's cousin, that
they did not really wish me to continue with the last part of

the book that Eric had not completed. I was free therefore to write a book about exploring with Eric and then bring it up to date with a new expedition in the Darwin Range and another visit to the Bridges at Viamonte and Harberton.

People often ask how long it takes to plan and prepare for an expedition. Eric used to say that most of the planning could be done on the back of an envelope in half an hour and indeed that is probably possible, especially if one knows an area. What takes the time are the seemingly endless letters that have to be written, permits and visas obtained and then the food and gear collected and packed. It is not the planning that is the main bugbear.

The plan that resolved itself was that with the help, once again, of the Chilean navy, I hoped to be dropped at the end of Parry Bay, a fiord that runs south, deep into the mountains of the Darwin Range from Admiralty Sound. Having landed there, I then hoped to make a traverse of the high glaciers across to the Stoppani Glacier and eventually end up at Yendegaia. I also hoped that it might be possible to attempt to climb Roncagli from the west or north-west, if that side proved easier than the south which Eric and I had seen from Bové and Francés. I made the various applications necessary through the Chilean Embassy in London. I visited the Chilean Naval Attaché who was extremely helpful and said that he would personally make contact with the Commander of the Third Naval Zone in Punta Arenas about our plans. Running parallel to this were all the similar arrangements I had to make with the Argentine Embassy, about the Bridges filming on the Argentine side of Tierra del Fuego. I met the Press Attaché, and had an interview with a Captain Gonzalez of the Naval Mission, who knew Tierra del Fuego well. They obviously needed to check my credentials and find out if, in fact, I really did know the branch of the Bridges family who lived there. Apparently I passed the test, for two most useful letters of introduction were sent to me by Captain Gonzalez, which later were to prove their worth.

Most important of all, I needed now to make up my party of two or three other members. This difficult and worrying task was a new one for me. On all my previous expeditions the responsibility of choosing the party had not been mine. I spoke and wrote to quite a number of my old climbing friends, many of whom had had previous expedition experience and were more or less the same age as myself. All of them, however, had jobs or other commitments that made it impossible for them to join me. At the same time, I had discussed the expedition with Iain Peters, a rock climber of great ability, and soon invited him to join me. I had known Iain, who was in his early thirties, for quite a number of years and he had been helping me with the running of my Outdoor Pursuits centre. He also had both theoretical and practical knowledge of the forestry industry and connections with Lord Bradford, who had been concerned with experiments with the nothofagus trees (the Southern beech) on his estates in Devon. So Iain was able to develop with the British Forestry Commission a programme of collecting seeds of the nothofagus, while we were in the remote parts of Tierra del Fuego, a valuable addition to the expedition.

It was several weeks before I was able to fill the other two places and the composition of the party caused me considerable anxiety. Finally I invited Dave Harber, another young rock climber in his early twenties to join us and only a few weeks before we were to leave, Don Sargeant became the fourth member of the party. Don, in his late twenties, had an art school background as an illustrator and was a very competent photographer, with some knowledge of film-making. It took a great load off my mind to have someone to help me with the filming.

The members of the expedition were settled at last and the food and gear began to accumulate at my Dartmoor home. I had tried to keep everything down to a basic minimum, but somehow the discipline slipped and the piles of food grew bigger and bigger and the mass of climbing gear looked unbelievable in comparison with the one rope, four pairs of crampons and four ice-axes that Eric and I had taken. Many firms had helped us, either by gifts or by letting us have their products at cost or trade price and with help from British Caledonian Airways and a grant from the Everest Foundation and the British Mountaineering Council, plus our own contributions, the financial side of the expedition looked fairly healthy.

Iain had arranged a farewell dinner and get-together in a pub on the northern edge of Dartmoor for people who had helped and who had an interest in the expedition. Much as I hated organised parties, I felt that it was a good idea and my wife, Pauline and I made our way over to Sticklepath on a cold December night. I was slightly taken aback to find the pub swarming with people whom I did not know, several from the hard, rock-climbing world, including quite a number of uninvited climbers who had got wind of the party! The dinner itself was excellent and fun, but I could not help a sneaking feeling that everything had slipped from my control when some unknown person asked who I was and why I was there!   At last we were off. I have faced customs with my camera gear all over the world; Bombay, Delhi, Algiers, Toronto. But it was with some trepidation that I now prepared to confront the Buenos Aires Customs, however, luck was with us. One of my many friends, who had helped us during the planning of the expedition, worked for ICI in the Americas and had put me in touch with the manager of Duperail, the Argentine subsidiary of ICI. He, in turn, had sent down one of his representatives to see us through the Customs. Naturally, I had papers for the camera gear, film stock and the expedition food and equipment, but "the less said the better" was the policy and unbelievably we were escorted through the Customs in thirty seconds! Never in my experience had I passed through so quickly, not even returning from Brittany from a holiday. Heaven knows how much it must have cost in bribes. Two cars were at our disposal and once again it was VIP treatment. As we drove the fifty kilometres into the city, the Duperail contact man, Juan, talked non-stop about what we should do and not do, the people we should see, and for the first time we now came face to face with major problems.

We had been aware back in Britain of the extremely tense political situation that existed between the Argentine and Chile over territorial claims in the Beagle Channel. It looked as if the two countries were poised on the brink of war and

Tierra del Fuego was a military zone. When I had asked Captain Gonzales how serious the situation was and whether there was anything he could suggest, he replied, "Well, you could always take a gun!" Now we began to experience the whole problem at first hand. Juan was most depressed and depressing about our continuing south to Tierra del Fuego. He thought it most unlikely that we should be allowed there, especially with camera gear. It appeared that the Argentine military government had declared an emergency, mobilised their forces and had bought a vast number of new planes and weapons. There had been air-raid practices in Buenos Aires and the whole country had been drummed up to fever pitch against Chile. There were severe restrictions of movement for civilians, especially along the border. Armed troops and police were evident everywhere.

The streets of Buenos Aires seemed very deserted, but we were astonished to see crowds of people in the windows of the high blocks of offices and business buildings, throwing armfuls of waste paper out into the streets below. The air was full of side-slipping sheets of note paper, computer print-outs, letters, account sheets all fluttering down. Juan explained that this was the usual way to behave on the last working day of the year. It appeared that all the waste paper of the previous year goes out of the window. It was indeed Friday, December 29th. Nobody worked on Saturdays, and Sunday was New Year's Eve. I could not help feeling sorry for the poor street cleaners who were already at work sweeping the paper up. I also wondered what on earth would happen if some vital documents got into the wrong pile and followed the rest, fluttering into the street. I had a splendid mental picture of worried secretaries, scrabbling about on hands and knees in the gutter on Monday morning.

The manager of Duperail had booked us into the huge City Hotel. It had a splendidly seedy, Victorian, slightly run-down feel, in many ways like some of the hotels I had stayed at in India, hotels of the Raj. For a while just after the war the City Hotel was considered to be the best in Buenos Aires. Now it gave the impression that it had seen better days. However, it was still very comfortable, not too expensive by international standards, and completely empty. Our major problem was the enormous amount of gear and equipment that we had with us. If we had had only ourselves and a rucksack each, we might well have moved to a cheaper, smaller hotel, but our fourteen heavy boxes and kit bags had been stowed safely in the basement and we were loath to move them again until we flew south.

In London we had booked our flight to Tierra del Fuego for the following day, so it was a bitter blow to learn that the Buenos Aires office of Aerolinas Argentinas had never heard of our London reservation and the earliest available seats south, for civilians anyway, were on a flight leaving on January 5th. It meant we had to hang around in this sweating, humid city with nothing to do and everything dead and closed for the New Year weekend, while our precious money trickled away paying for the hotel and for meals.

Mostly we ate frugally from back-street shops but on New Year's Eve we were forced to eat in the hotel for there was nothing else open. The huge dining room, complete with candelabra and dusty red velvet drapes was absolutely empty. We huddled in one corner where we were served by disconsolate waiters. The meal cost us £34.00. In our hotel bedroom we attacked the duty-free whisky!

At ten minutes to midnight we decided to go out. In the distance, down at the docks, ships' sirens and hooters were sounding and even a few flares and fireworks went up, but the streets themselves were almost completely deserted. A few people walked about grimly. Iain had found out the Spanish for "Happy New Year" and he went along shaking the hands of the few astonished passers-by, trying out his Spanish. Some of them responded and smiled at this friendly gesture. At the far end of the square, with the Cathedral on one side, was a large pink building and most of the festivities seemed to be going on beyond, down at the docks. The broad pavement that ran along one side of this pink palace looked as though it should lead to a good vantage point, and we had started to walk along it when suddenly a very young soldier leapt out at us with a machine gun. "Happy New Year", said Iain. "English", I said. The young man gestured angrily with his gun. Foolishly we took another step forward. Being held up at gun point is not an experience one is used to and it was hard to believe that it was happening to us. Suddenly I sensed that terrible fear in the young soldier. His sweating face shone green in the street lights, his eyes were flicking wildly from one to another of us. He was terrified out of his wits, and frightened, cornered men are at their most dangerous. I believe we all came very close to being shot on that New Year's Eve, 1978. We had acted foolishly and unthinkingly. We had not appreciated fully what life is like in a country run by a military government and ruled by fear and strict control; where the man with the gun is superior and always right. A plain-clothes man with a revolver also moved out from the shadows by the main door of the building. Without another word we turned and walked away, dry mouthed and hearts pounding. We each had a tickling sensation in the hair at the back of our necks; we knew the guns were still pointing at us. We discovered later that the pink building was the palace where Eva Peron used to speak to the crowds from the balcony.

One incident did relieve the utter despair and sadness of that New Year's Eve. When we eventually got back to the hotel after wandering the empty streets, I went to have a shower. Iain followed me into the bathroom and we were discussing the bidet that was installed there. I was explaining how it worked, and we both leant forward to get a better view. I turned the tap to demonstrate and the jet of water squirted with a mighty swoosh into our faces! We both laughed and laughed until the sound echoed down the dusty, empty corridors of the City Hotel. January 1st, 1979, and at least there had been laughter eventually.

Only once more did we come face to face with repressive authority. Stories of imprisonment without trial, police and military brutality and torture were rife, and in order to protest about the disappearance of people without trace in the Argentine, mothers, wives and relatives would meet and stand silently outside the Cathedal in the square near our hotel. Iain and Dave saw the gathering in the square and the large numbers of police and military in attendance. It was obviously an emotional and nervous time for all concerned. The atmosphere was electric and one felt that any false step could have ended in riot and, without doubt, shooting. Iain and Dave had their cameras with them and again, unthinkingly, as one would have done in Britain, felt they would like to photograph the incident. No sooner had they raised their cameras, than they were surrounded with uniformed and plain-clothes police, all naturally armed. Their cameras were seized, but later returned. Again it was a disturbing incident and the aspect that worried me was the fact that we all had BBC Television stamped in the visas on our passports. After the controversy over the screening of a highly critical Panorama programme about the Argentine, I did not want to be involved in any backlash from that.

After the bank holiday our Embassy was able to arrange an interview for us with the Press Department of the Argentine Foreign Office which went a long way to relieving my anxieties. Far from restrictions being put on our movements in Tierra del Fuego, they were very anxious that I *should* film at Ushuaia, the Argentine naval base in the Beagle Channel. Our temporary accommodation problem solved itself most happily at the same time. Dave had only his climbing boots with him for foot gear, so had been clumping round town in these in the appalling heat, but because of them he was identified in the street as a fellow climber by a young man who belonged to a group of Buenos Aires-based Argentine climbers, and he and Iain were immediately offered somewhere to stay. They had fellow climbers to talk to and even a chance one day to go climbing and abseiling on a motorway bridge, the only place where the climbers of Buenos Aires can practise. Don and I meanwhile had contacted and been invited to stay with the Watzls, old friends of Phyllis Wint and Eric Shipton. Gerardo Watzl was an Austrian Argentinian and a fine mountaineer who had been on the first Argentine expedition to Dhaulagiri.

This was the time that the Pope had been called in to try and avert war between the Argentine and Chile. We saw the cardinal he had appointed as mediator several times in Buenos Aires being driven in a heavily-armed motorcade to the airport as he commuted between Buenos Aires and Santiago. The other interesting encounter we had was an invitation to cocktails with the Residency Chargé d'Affaires,

The main Bridges family house at Harberton.

Looking north from Harberton up into the mountains through which Lucas Bridges built his track to Viamonte.

Above left: Thomas Bridges, aged 25, when he sailed to England for the first time to be ordained, and met and married Mary Ann Varder in Harberton, Devon.

Above right: Mary Bridges in old age. She was carried in a sedan chair by Ona Indians from Harberton to Viamonte over the new track, but eventually returned to England and is buried in the village churchyard at Shipbourne, Kent.

A group of Ona Indians whom Lucas Bridges encountered at Harberton.

Hugh Carless, who had, of course, been Eric Newby's partner on the famous journey chronicled so hilariously in *A Short Walk in the Hindu Kush*.

At last the waiting was over and we were on our way with our 270 kilograms of baggage – checked in amazingly as only 130 kilograms. Could it have been the airport scales? Our first stop was at Rio Gallegos on the south-east tip of mainland Argentina. Here Iain was going to leave us to travel overland, he hoped, by a ramshackle coach service called Il Penguino, with all the climbing expedition food and equipment, over the border into Chile and on to Punta Arenas. While Don, Dave and I were filming at Viamonte and Harberton, Iain had an appointment to keep with Captain John Howard, who was the Commander of the Third Chilean Naval zone in Punta Arenas. Although we had not heard from him ourselves, Captain Kenneth Pugh, the Naval Attaché in London, had kept him fully informed of our plans, and we thought that all Iain had to do now was to tie up the final arrangements for our transport to the Darwin Range. Iain also had to meet various representatives of the Chilean Forestry Department, who were expecting him, to discuss his plans for seed collecting. We all felt slightly apprehensive for Iain, in spite of assurances by everyone that all was more or less normal now. Clearly, Rio Gallegos was very much a military zone, with armed guards everywhere, fighter aircraft taking off and landing and anti-aircraft guns around the perimeter. On take-off for Rio Grande and the flight across the Magellan Straits, we were told to pull down the blinds of the aircraft's windows. The thought of Iain struggling over what was virtually a front line, from Argentine to Chile, with all the gear, was depressing.

However Iain was not on his own. With amazing good fortune, one of his contacts, Dr. David Moore from Reading University, a man who knew the area well and was now actively engaged on research and seed collecting himself, had been on the same flight. It was with great relief that we had seen the two walk across the tarmac together to the airport buildings.

We made a long, low approach through mist and cloud,

over the sea to Rio Grande, stepping out into a cool drizzle, a blessed contrast with Buenos Aires. The way to the airport building was lined with armed guards. We were herded into a waiting area at gun point and then had to queue to pass through another identity and passport control, where we were given a form to fill in. On the other side of the control we were one again herded into a waiting area, still at gun point. It was an unpleasant and alien experience. To us it seemed quite extraordinary that the military should treat their own people in this repressive way. It was almost as if Argentina was an occupied country and that these were occupying troops, inflicting tight control over the civilians they felt might turn into resistance forces at any moment. But the more one heard and read about the situation in the Argentine, the more one realised that in fact, in many ways, this was exactly the situation.

Apparently no civilians were allowed to drive to the airport to collect friends arriving by air; it was a military zone, but all we saw were a few anti-aircraft guns around the field and fighters parked on the far side of the tarmac. We waited resentfully for an hour and a half in the hallway of the airport building, before there was room in the coach into town. All our baggage, including, of course, my camera gear, was taken on a separate vehicle. At last we stepped out of the coach into the main street of Rio Grande. Oliver Bridges moved out of the crowd to welcome us. Time slipped away; it seemed only a short while, instead of sixteen years, since he had welcomed Eric, Phyllis and myself. He had not changed at all in appearance and his instant kindness and friendliness and, above all, his calmness brought a sense of relief for me. We were here and Oliver assured me that there were no problems. Most of the rumours about the situation that had percolated through to Buenos Aires had indeed been exaggerated, misleading, perhaps even deliberately. Filming could start as soon as we were ready and we had discussed the plans with the family.

10

Thomas Bridges of Tierra del Fuego

For just under three weeks, Don, Dave and I were looked
after by Betsy and Oliver Bridges at their small house near
the main estancia of Viamonte. In spite of the fact that many
of the Chilean workers had been forced out of the Argentine
side of Tierra del Fuego back to Punta Arenas, by niggling,
bureaucratic regulations, Betsy still had her cook to help her
with the running of the house. The cook's husband also
helped with the work, especially cutting and bringing wood
to keep the various wood-burning stoves and fires going.
Even the bath water was heated by a wood-burning stove
actually in the bathroom itself, with a water jacket around it.
It heated the water incredibly quickly and, of course,
warmed the room in moments.

In spite of some food being in short supply, we ate well
with huge three-, even four-course meals at midday and in
the evening. One evening a ten-pound sea trout had been
netted in the mouth of the river and it was prepared for us.
There was always plenty of excellent Argentine wine and
Betsy, on our second evening there, insisted on preparing a
welcoming Black Velvet, made from Argentine Champagne

131

and Guinness bottled in Buenos Aires! We all felt ourselves putting on more and more weight and growing more and more unfit. All the running on Dartmoor and carrying heavy rucksacks for long walks before I had left were of no avail. My paunch hung over my trousers and I panted heavily, walking up slight inclines!

We had a couple of splendidly relaxed days wandering through the nothofagus forests near Viamonte, getting rid of the sour atmosphere of Buenos Aires and the previous week of frustrating inactivity. In the forests, many of the old trees were gnarled and twisted into contorted shapes, the grey branches festooned with green and yellow hair-like lichens, streaming and flowing in the constant wind. We came across several old corrals and ruined wooden buildings, all made of the dry, hard, grey, nothofagus trunks. On the vast rolling, open camps, as they called the fields, where many trees had been burnt and removed, we saw cattle, mainly Herefords, and sheep, in large numbers. The cattle were shy and wild and when we accidentally stampeded them they thundered off with their tails held high. Later we heard that if fresh meat was wanted they had to go out and shoot the cattle, almost as if hunting big game in Africa.

During one of our walks, four very old bi-plane fighters flew low over the forest. As we had the tripod and camera with us, we hid like naughty schoolboys caught in the act; the experiences of the previous week had made us wary.

Oliver, in his gentle, quiet way, discussed with me the filming plans I had in mind and we soon had a programme worked out. I needed to visit various locations in Tierra del Fuego that had a historical significance in the story of the Bridges and their settlement there. Then I needed to interview the various members of the family, who lived and worked at Viamonte and Harberton. Finally I needed sequences of the work being carried out on the estancias, as well as scenic shots of places of interest. In spite of the fact that Oliver had considerable work concerned with the overall administration of the family Company, of which he is chairman, and also needed to take a holiday while he was down in Tierra del Fuego, he put himself entirely at our disposal. During the next two weeks, he drove us to many locations, travelling vast distances over the rough, rolling tracks cut through the forest. He organised many of the activities we wanted to film.

We travelled to Ushuaia in two pick-up trucks, Oliver driving ahead in one and myself at the wheel of the other. A new road was being built from Rio Grande to Ushuaia, cutting off many of the corners of the old one. The surface however was still untarmacked and deeply rutted in places with long ridges of loose gravel. I found the pick-up quite a handful to control, as it had a very light tail and I had several hair-raising skids and swerves in the dense clouds of dust from Oliver's truck ahead of me.

Clarita Goodall, Oliver's sister who was now seventy-seven years old, travelled with me and she talked a lot of the time, remembering little anecdotes brought to mind by the sight of certain sections of the forest or road or distant hills. She remembered, with absolute clarity, as elderly people often do, incidents that happened when she was a girl, when she was with her father, William, one of the sons of Thomas and Mary Bridges. She recalled how she was caught in a severe snow storm when out with her father deep in the trackless forest and how he had cut long strips of wood from the nothofagus and made primitive skis to carry them over the deep snow back to Harberton. She remembered a little hut at the far extremities of the Viamonte land, where, as children, they had stayed on holidays, living rough and cooking for themselves. As with Aunty Bertha, whom I met sixteen years before and who sadly was now dead, I found it hard to believe that this gentle, little, old lady was so tough and full of practical common sense about survival and living in this windswept land.

The character of the countryside changes beyond Lake Fagnano, known to the Indians as Kami. The lake is over sixty miles long, but narrow; a deep, fiorded valley that is almost a continuation of Admiralty Sound. The north and east of Tierra del Fuego is a dry, rolling plain, but at Lake Fagnano the mountains began to crowd the water's edge, clothed in dense, dark green nothofagus trees. Two conical mountains stand on the northern shore called the Paint Mountains. The Ona Indians used to dig out coloured minerals from these to daub their bodies as a sign of mourning, or sometimes for hunting camouflage they would smear their bodies and their bows and quivers – yellow when hunting in withered grass, and white for snow conditions. After the flatness of Buenos Aires and even Viamonte I was thrilled to be back in the mountains. The steep Garibaldi Pass had a fine, new, easy-gradient road cut up it and the summit had a large car-park where tourists could stop and look back over Kami. It was very different from the tortuous zig-zags I had driven up on my first visit to Harberton sixteen years before.

Ushuaia was still packed with Argentine marines who had requisitioned the local school and several other buildings for barracks. We had heard that there had been over fifteen thousand marines in Tierra del Fuego at one time at the height of the troubles. I still had the uneasy feeling of being in an occupied country and filmed in the main street with caution and in a surreptitious way, expecting to be hustled off at gun point any moment. We stayed, as Oliver's guests, at a modern hotel run by the Argentine Automobile Club, which was completely empty except for marine and naval officers relaxing during their off-duty hours. The tourist industry had been very badly hit by the conflict, and many of the small shop and hotel owners had packed up and left for the north, in fear of bombing raids by the Chileans, which indeed were most unlikely as most of the aggression had come, in fact, from the Argentine. That evening, however, a squat, red, powerful-looking vessel edged into the dock and tied up near the large naval supply and troop carrier and the fast naval torpedo launches. It looked out of place in this military setting. It was the *Limblad Explorer*, a cruise ship that calls in regularly during the summer on trips along the Beagle Channel and down to the Antarctic. All was hustle

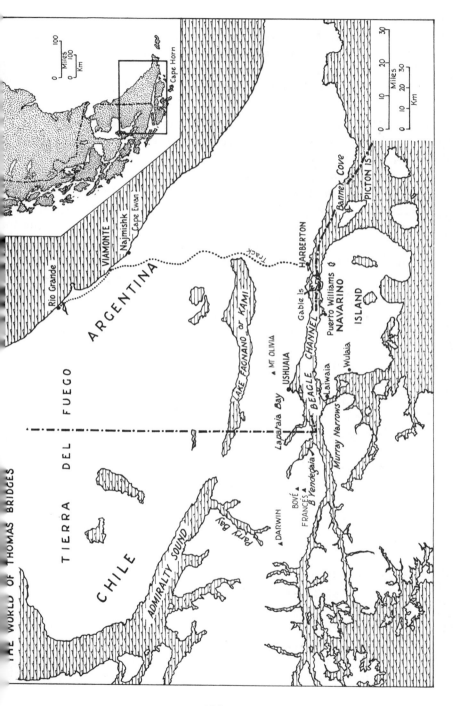

THE WORLD OF THOMAS BRIDGES

135

and bustle as the tourists, mainly Americans, had just arrived by coach from Rio Grande, and were now making their way on board. To my astonishment, I met among them Sir Peter Scott and Keith Shackleton, both of whom I had last met at the BBC canteen in Bristol.

In Ushuaia itself the local government building was very modern and exciting; all triangles and points echoing the jagged surrounding peaks. The main street was broad but the buildings were mainly single storeyed corrugated iron, nearly all of them small shops aimed at tourists, with souvenirs mass-produced in Buenos Aires. I could see or buy nothing that was a product and true souvenir of Tierra del Fuego; but this is a fault that occurs all over the world, including my own village of Widecombe-in-the-Moor. Most of the people either work in the naval dockyards, in the crab-canning plants, or, in the very brief season, with the tourist industry. There were a few better-built houses on the outskirts, homes of the estancia owners, or naval officers. But take away the navy and military and one felt that there would be little left. I found Ushuaia a depressing, unfriendly place.

The following day we set out westwards along a delight-ful, scenic road that led into the National Park a few miles from Ushuaia. The track was very dusty, and wound along the side of the river that had cut down into a deep gorge. The lower slopes of the hills were littered with the grey stumps of trees; it looked for all the world like a battlefield. Oliver later told me that the trees had been felled years ago for fuel by convicts at a penal settlement. By some very beautiful lakes and a bay called Lapataia we were very close to the border with Chile and almost unbelievably only fifteen miles from Estancia Yendegaia where we hoped to reach later on our climbing expedition. However, Oliver had made it very clear in his letters to me that it would be impossible to pass from the Argentine to Chile this way at this particular time. But how tantalising to be so close to the mountains we had come to explore. Indeed, from Lapataia we could see Bové that I had climbed with Eric and, further north, looking very steep and difficult, Roncagli and other big snow peaks. Clouds and storms wreathed their summits and I had a strange shiver of anticipation and apprehension at the thought of getting to grips with them in a few weeks' time.

On the way back we stopped at a point where I could film a view of Ushuaia with Mount Olivia in the background. It was lucky that Oliver was with me, for no sooner had I taken the shot than two armed marines materialised from nowhere. We had not noticed that all along the hill slope and on the tops of the low hills, there were anti-aircraft gun emplacements.

Oliver now took me to the long arm of land that encloses the bay on the south of Ushuaia. The main town lies on the north side of the bay, but here on this peninsula, just above some houses built for naval officers, stands an historic monument. It is found almost at the highest point of a field of long coarse grass and it is an upended, triangular concrete slab, painted white. It was on this spot that Stirling House stood, the five-roomed bungalow of wood and corrugated iron that was the very first home of Thomas and Mary Bridges in Tierra del Fuego. We were visiting the starting point of the history of the Bridges family in Tierra del Fuego.

The incredible voyage of the *Beagle* with Captain Fitzroy and Charles Darwin on board, and the subsequent bringing of the Yahgan Indians, Jemmy Button, York Minster and Fuegia Basket back to Britain, are now all a well-known part of history. So indeed is the fanatical missionary work of Allen Gardiner in Tierra del Fuego, that ended in death for himself and for his party after appalling hardship and hideous suffering. But the Patagonian Missionary Society Gardiner had founded did not give up. A new mission was established on Keppel Island in the Falklands, from which comparatively safe base further overtures were made to the Fuegeans, with the hapless Jemmy Button pressed into the role of go-between. It was a sorry story, without much show of Christian charity within the mission itself, and the venture

received its apparent death blow in a massacre at Wulaia on
the Murray Narrows in 1859, which some said was instigated
by the wretched Jemmy Button. For the mission leader, the
Reverend Pakenham Despard, it was the end, and he proposed to London that they should abandon any further
attempts to establish a mission in Tierra del Fuego.

When the Reverend Pakenham Despard had arrived at
Keppel Island in 1856, he had had with him his adopted son,
Thomas Bridges, then a boy of thirteen. During the years
that followed, the boy played with the Fuegan children at the
mission and, like many young people, he was able to pick up
their language with ease, coupled with the fact that he
obviously had a very good ear for languages. By the time of
the massacre he was almost completely fluent in Yahgan. It
took two years before Despard received word from the
Missionary Society that they agreed to his returning home,
and when he left he took back with him almost everyone
who had come out from Britain originally. Only one person
remained and that was the young Thomas Bridges, now
eighteen years old.

For over a year, the only other people left at Keppel
were an Indian called George Okkoko and his wife. To
Thomas Bridges this was an incredible opportunity to
improve his knowledge of their language, not only the way it
was spoken but also the complicated grammar. It was at this
time that he started his famous Yahgan dictionary that rests
now in the British Museum. How it eventually found its way
there is yet another story.

The next step was obviously to sail to the windswept
Yahgan lands to the west about which he had been told so
many exciting stories but which the Reverend Pakenham
Despard had never allowed him to visit. In 1863 Bridges and
a newly-arrived missionary, the Reverend W. H. Stirling,
made the first voyage together to the Beagle Channel and
Wulaia. For young Bridges it must have been a moving and
momentous journey and one which was to have a profound
influence on the rest of his life. The Indians were at first
completely taken aback at being spoken to in their own

tongue by a white man. No doubt because of this Stirling and Bridges received a friendly welcome.

During the next five years Bridges made a great many journeys from the Falklands to the Beagle Channel. One of the main purposes was to establish a settlement for the Yahgans on Navarino Island at a place called Laiwaia, near the entrance of the Murray Narrows. He provided them with potatoes, goats and fences and introduced them to the idea of farming to augment their hunting and gathering of shellfish.

Bridges' other aim, however, was to establish a more accessible permanent mission station. On the northern shore of the Beagle Channel he found the sheltered harbour known by the Yahgans as Ushuaia, or "inner harbour to the west-ward". Nearby, was a small coastal plain, suitable for cultivation. It seemed an ideal spot. The establishment of the mission station was a comparative success and gradually the Yahgans began to settle permanently in the area and clear the land. It must, however, have been a lonely and risky venture. One of the Yahgan members of the crew of the vessel that returned later said to Stirling, "I am very glad. I think my countrymen kill you, but you have wigwams all round your home."

In 1868 Thomas Bridges was summoned to Britain to be ordained and while there he met Mary Varder, the young schoolteacher from Harberton in Devon. They fell in love and within five weeks were married in the little granite church. Two days later they sailed for Keppel Island, and two years later, with their eight-month-old daughter, Mary, they set sail again from Keppel for Ushuaia. It was a terrible voyage. Towering seas poured for days on and over the little eighty-eight ton schooner as it was driven backward and forward four times through the Strait of Le Maire. Almost too weak to stand, and her face pale and strained with the rigours of sea-sickness, Mary whispered, "Dearest, you have brought me to this country and here I must remain; for I can never, never face that voyage again."

Four days later, they reached Ushuaia and together they walked up the rough track to where two little houses stood.

This was to be Mary's first home in the land where she was to live for most of her life. It was no wonder that Oliver Bridges found this spot so tremendously significant and moving, as he and I stood gazing out at the small modern town of Ushuaia. When Mary and Thomas first looked at the same view just over a hundred years before, there would have been only a few wigwams made of branches and turf along the shore and, scattered outside them, huge piles of mussel shells and other refuse. A pall of smoke drifting up through the wigwams would have been whipped away by the raw winds. The Yahgans would have been squatting, partly naked or clothed in otter skins, outside their huts. Beyond, the forests rose thick and impenetrable to the snow line and above that the jagged peaks reared into the grey sky. Only that part of the scene had not changed. Oliver and I turned and walked down the hill to the waiting truck.

From Ushuaia we were to visit Harberton and once again we set off in convoy. The track had much improved during the sixteen years since I had last followed it and there were now bridges where we had forded rivers before, and new sections of road built where there had been none. Harberton had not changed at all, except that there appeared to be a few more oil drums lying around. It is a most marvellous setting. The track leads over the neck of a narrow peninsula, below a low, round hill, past a massive corral and sturdy fences of seasoned grey nothofagus. Then we were running along the shore of Harberton Inlet, with its high-tide mark of bleached driftwood, mussel shells and kelp. The buildings were strung out along the shore line; the workers' bungalows, the shearing sheds and storage huts, and finally the house itself with its brick foundations, white corrugated iron walls, red roof and peeling, green-painted windows and doors. Walking in under an arch of whale bones on to the creaking veranda and into the hall was like walking into a Victorian vicarage. Ahead was the staircase and on the left the main living room with its comfortable easy chairs and the usual, wood-burning iron stove. On the far side, most incongruously, stood the mass of radio equipment that Tommy Goodall used to keep in touch with Viamonte and other estancias. Tommy, Clarita's second son, was the fourth generation of Bridges to live and farm at Harberton, but with the remoteness and the difficulties of getting sufficient labour to run the farm, it is likely that the way of life may change for the next generations.

Because of the fame of Thomas Bridges and his family, more and more people make what is almost a pilgrimage, to visit Harberton. Its setting is unique and incredibly beautiful and tranquil. Who knows but that, as well as running the farm on more restricted lines, future generations of Bridges may offer accommodation and holidays to travellers who wish to escape for a while from the rush of their normal busy lives and re-live again the solitude and peace that Thomas and Mary Bridges knew when they first arrived here.

The events which led Thomas Bridges to take the big step from mission-builder to rancher and estancia-builder were sorry ones, but perhaps inevitable. With Ushuaia a peaceful and growing settlement, the Argentine navy arrived in 1884 to establish Argentine rule in the person of a sub-prefect and twenty-one men. By this time the Bridges had six children and they and the other members of the mission lived and worked together amicably enough with the new administration. It had taken twelve years to gain the confidence of the Yahgan and to establish a thriving community based on Christian beliefs. But Bridges realised, as others before him, that primitive people so often pick up the bad habits of civilisation and this could undermine all that he had striven for.

In fact disaster came sooner than even he had anticipated. Only a few weeks after the Argentine ships had sailed away, an epidemic of measles raged through Ushuaia and the nearby islands. The Yahgans, with no inbuilt immunity to the worst effects of the disease, died in large numbers. It must have been a terrible time for Bridges and his family watching their friends dying, as die they did, over fifty per

.cent of them. They were not able to dig the graves quickly enough and each night Thomas would arrive back home exhausted from the heart-breaking work. The corpses lay scattered round the settlement and outside the wigwams. In one Yahgan family, everyone died except an infant who was cared for by the Bridges. Within ten years, only three hundred Yahgans remained alive from a population of three thousand. When I had called at Hoste Island in 1963, I had met the last surviving Yahgan, Grandmother Chachon. Now there are none. A whole race had been exterminated in under one hundred years.

It was this disaster, coupled with a rejection of his plans for the future of the mission at Ushuaia, which made Thomas Bridges take one more bold step in his forceful and dynamic life. Clearly the mission was doomed and he had now the responsibility of a wife and six children. In spite of the fact that he had very little financial backing and was a sick man, Bridges resigned from his post and determined to establish a ranch of his own in Tierra del Fuego. The Missionary Society in righteous indignation accused him of being "instigated by the Evil·One to his ruin", but at least the President of Argentina, President Roca, took a more Christian view and, valuing Bridges for what he had done for Tierra del Fuego, granted him the 50,000 acres of land he requested at a spot on the Beagle Channel the Yahgans called Tuwujlumbiwaia, which means Black Heron Bay.

Next, Thomas Bridges sailed for England, where he used all his savings to buy everything he would need to start his new life: bricks, coal, prefabricated wooden frames for a new house, flour, sugar, a South Devon bull, four Romney Marsh rams, two pigs and two sheepdogs. He chartered a brigantine called the *Shepherdess*, and returned to the Beagle Channel. With tremendous business drive, he then used the vessel to transport posts to the treeless Falkland Islands and exchanged them for three hundred sheep and seventy cattle. In April 1887, the family moved to Black Heron Bay and began to build Harberton. The fact that the original buildings still stand today has much to say not only for the workmanship of

Mary's father back in Devon, who put together the prefabricated frames, but also for that of Thomas and his growing sons.

It was some seven years before it became apparent that the venture was a success. Seven years of back-breaking hard work, always up against the harsh environment and the climate with its winters of heavy snow and short daylight hours, and the gales and storms of the summer. The whole venture hung in the balance between success and failure, but in the end the family won. In 1898, on his way to Buenos Aires with a cargo, Thomas Bridges died. This small, tireless man, who had never been afraid of hard work, danger and risk, had lived from the age of thirteen in this harsh, cruel, yet haunting part of the world. And he had devoted his life utterly to the Yahgans and his family and by this devotion had preached the Christian way of life far more effectively than any sermon or writing could have done, simply by his example. Mary must have been utterly desolated by his death, yet she found enormous strength from the knowledge of what they had achieved together. He might be dead, but his influence, his physical and mental strength and his faith lived on in his children. Indeed, when he had been very ill he had said, "I live in my children."

Don, Dave and I spent idyllic days filming at Harberton. Once we walked along the shore past the large grass-covered mounds of mussel shells that marked the old Yahgan encampments. It was a still sunny day with a blue sky. Beyond a wind-bleached whale skeleton, we reached the Beagle Channel and there, hovering above the calm water, we could see again the two great snow peaks of Bové and Francés over seventy miles away to the west. As we walked back, dolphins swam parallel to the shore, leaping out of the water in sheer joy at the golden day.

One sequence I needed was to film parts of the old track that ran north from Harberton to Lake Fagnano and on to Viamonte. I would have dearly loved to walk it myself, but it is not clearly marked now, trees have fallen across it and beavers have dammed streams and flooded large sections of the land across which it used to pass. (The beaver, of course, is not an animal indigenous to Tierra del Fuego but was introduced by a governor only a short while back. Since then it has run wild and caused chaos, by damming streams and flooding valleys, which makes it almost impossible to travel overland on foot).

The story of the Bridges' track is fascinating. Thomas had tried several times, when he was at Ushuaia, to penetrate into the interior of Tierra del Fuego. He had heard rumours of a large lake and he wanted to meet and find out more about the elusive Ona, the third tribe of Fuegean Indians. But his few attempts were failures. It was Lucas Bridges, his second son, who finally succeeded. Lucas had much of the pioneering and far-seeing drive of his father. All through his youth he had known the Yahgans, and, like his father, had been intrigued by the mysterious land beyond the mountains and the sinister presence of the Ona. At Harberton he had often been aware of the Ona, though he had never seen the shadowy nomadic hunters who stole through the forest. Horrifying stories came through to him of fatal encounters between the Ona and the settlers and miners in the north and east of Tierra del Fuego, where white men were attempting to make a living on what was Ona territory. Like his father, he made several attempts to penetrate the forests and mountains to the north of Harberton. On one occasion he and his brothers found a large Ona camp and traces of fire, but no sign of the people. Often, though, they had the hair-prickling sensation of being watched when moving about their work in the forest.

The first contact came in 1894 when Lucas was twenty years old. One evening two Indians emerged from the forest, when Lucas was alone with his two younger sisters. He put down his rifle and walked towards the Indians. The Ona also put down their bows and quivers and for a while the three sat on the ground and tried to talk. Their language was completely different from that of the Yahgan and he could not understand a word, but it was obvious by their gestures and gentle speech that they wished to be friendly. After a while

Getting about the Bridges estancia: *above*, rounding up the sheep by traditional methods; *below* Adrian Goodall and his lovingly preserved Royal Enfield at Viamonte.

Above left: a Yahgan skull unearthed at Puerto Williams, on the shore of the Beagle Channel. *Above right:* the author suffering the ten miles from Yendegaia to the Stoppani Glacier, his feet trailing the ground, and the horse bolting at the sound of the film camera.

An old boat at Yendegaia that was not going to get us anywhere.

they left. The next day, he met a group of twenty of them and again they were friendly. Later the same day a whole party appeared at Harberton, including women and children, who stayed for several days. This was the start. By 1896 the Ona were making regular visits to Harberton and staying for long periods. Lucas also travelled with them on hunting trips that took him at last up into the mountains to the north of Harberton and into the unknown land that he had dreamt of visiting as a child.

Three years later came the chance to carry out the exploration that his father had attempted and that he had also yearned to do. Travelling with the Ona, with their strange gliding stride, he had climbed out of the forest into the barren hills beyond and up to the rocky summits. The route they had followed twisted and turned to avoid the rivers, bogs and cliffs and then for the first time Lucas Bridges stood and looked down on the great lake about which his father had heard rumours. This was Lake Kami, now known as Lake Fagnano. But the journey was not over and Lucas, with his seven Ona friends, pushed on down to the pampas and the undulating country to the east until they reached the Rio Grande. The settlers there were astounded to see this young man emerge from the forests of the south, which they knew were inhabited only by the murderous Ona.

It was after this amazing journey that the Ona began to suggest, most emphatically, that Lucas should move from Harberton and start a ranch in the flat pampas lands to the north-east. The Ona had watched the encroachment of the white man into their country, and had seen him put a price on their heads. They felt if Lucas were to settle in their land they would have a refuge where they could continue their nomadic life without fear of being shot at or having their hunting grounds taken from them. Lucas knew enough of the world to know that you cannot hold back the inevitable, but after the family's experience with the Yahgans he was determined to help the Ona adapt to a changing world. He decided to move east and teach them farming.

His brothers' initial opposition to the plan was worn down

and eventually they agreed that he could opt out of his work at Harberton and devote all his time to establishing the new ranch, and if it was a success the whole family would then unite again to share the profits.

The first task was to cut a track over which Lucas could travel easily to the new area and eventually drive stock. In a straight line, the distance from Harberton to Najmishk, the site Lucas had chosen on the east coast about thirty miles south of Rio Grande, was some fifty miles. When the track was cut, it covered almost twice that distance, and took two years to complete, through dense forest and scrub, with causeways of tree trunks built over the worst areas of marsh. Finally, in 1902, Lucas left Harberton with forty-two pack horses carrying over a ton of building materials and provisions. It took four days to reach Najmishk where, with the help of a Welshman called Dan Prewitt, he built a one-roomed shack, which they named Viamonte. This was where Lucas and the Welshman lived for five years.

Don, Dave and I followed the first stages of the track that wound up the hills near Harberton. We climbed to a ridge where we could look back at the little cluster of white buildings beside the bay, with the Beagle Channel and Navarino Island beyond. Looking north we could see the distant mountains, Pink Mountain, Mount Spion Kop, over which the track wound.

Before we finally left Harberton I filmed Tommy's wife, Natalie, at work in the garden boiling up bones of dolphins (to remove any traces of flesh) that she had collected along the beaches of Tierra del Fuego. She had become intrigued with these small whales and by collecting the skeletons of creatures that had become stranded and died, she is accumulating an immense amount of knowledge about them. She has a grant from the National Geographic Society for this work. It struck me that the women of the estancias, unless they were actively involved in the farming, needed something to occupy their time and their minds in this remote, cut-off world. Clarita, for instance, in spite of the hard work of running Harberton, first with her father, Will, and later with her husband, found time to produce, over the years, exquisite water colour paintings of the wild flowers of Tierra del Fuego. On the back of each painting is the Latin name, the English or Spanish name, and the name the Indians called the flower, together with an account of the occasion when she first found the flower; charming, personal information and anecdotes that make the collection very much more than just a catalogue.

A week later we paid a visit to Najmishk, Viamonte, with Adrian Goodall, Clarita's other son, who is now the manager of New Viamonte. We rattled our way along the coast on a very rough track through the forest. On several occasions we had to get out and push away or cut up trees that had fallen across our path. The Land-Rover that Adrian was driving was the one that I had travelled in on my first trip to Harberton sixteen years before, still going strong, if a little erratically! Both Adrian and Tommy have to be experts at car maintenance. Spare parts and garages for repairs are very few and far between. Adrian also runs a splendid old Royal Enfield motorbike that he uses to travel across country, checking stock and fences. We reached the top of a drop and could see below us a steep track cut out of the side of a hill. Adrian cheerfully told us that he had gone over the edge in one of the pick-ups a few weeks ago and then he set off down the hill pumping hard at the brakes!

We could see why Lucas had chosen this spot for his ranch. Behind the site the forest thinned naturally and the huge area of flat grasslands stretched along the coast to Cape Ewan. Yet there was enough forest around for fuel and building materials. Nothing very much is now left of Lucas's "hut in Ona land". There were a few wooden foundations, a fence, the remains of a corral. But here he prospered and eventually was able to secure the title to 254,000 acres of land. He also managed to get the warring tribes of the Ona to stop their feuds, by taking part in an ancient ceremony called Jelj.

But the ever restless Lucas, still full of pioneering drive, planned yet another venture and move. Harberton had become too small for the expanding families. The hut at Najmishk could not accommodate anyone else, so he planned a grand new settlement. This was about twelve miles further north along the coast towards the Rio Grande. It was to have a huge shearing shed, a saw mill, accommodation for some of the family from Harberton and, of course, the Ona workers that he now employed. So the present Viamonte was constructed by the family.

In 1910 Mary Bridges, who was then sixty-eight, left Harberton for the last time. She was carried over the track that her son Lucas had cut in the mysterious Fuegean wilderness, on a special sedan chair, by Ona Indians. It took six days to reach Viamonte. At the highest point of the track she looked back towards the Beagle Channel. What a flood of memories and thoughts must have rushed past her. This was where she had lived for forty years. She must have remembered her arrival with her dynamic husband, his faith, courage and hard work, that had brought to her and their sons and daughters prosperity and security, the very thing that Thomas had wished for. She was never to return to Harberton again. She lived at Viamonte for three years and then finally returned to England where she died in 1922, at the age of eighty.

As for the Ona, for a while they prospered in and around Viamonte, and became skilled at shepherding, shearing and fencing. As most of the work was seasonal, they were able to melt away when it was finished and live as traditional nomadic hunters, deep in the forests. But in spite of Lucas Bridges' care and concern, once again it was measles that finally destroyed this proud race and now, like the Yahgan they are no more.

When Don, Dave and I returned to Viamonte from Harberton we had quite a number of sequences to film which kept us busy, but, as always, it was so often the little events, situations, conversations, that we could not film, that gave the truest insights. The cameras, lights, tape recorders and the whole intruding rigmarole of film-making often destroy the intimacy that comes out of ordinary conversations. At Harberton, Clarita had opened a box of treasures to show us. There had been bills, accounts, letters, quill pens, arrowheads and even a Bill of Sale for a boat called *Phantom*, which Thomas Bridges had bought in Porthmadog in North Wales. At Viamonte I discovered that one of Aunty Bertha's sons, known to everyone as Beetle, had been to a prep school in Tonbridge, Kent, which I knew well. We sat and talked, remembering things together about the area and enjoying that marvellous contact that comes when people share common knowledge. Beetle and I also share a sense of humour that verges on the slightly vulgar and ridiculous. Perhaps it had been the talk of prep schools that had set us off!

Beetle had been one of the first people to fly a private plane in Tierra del Fuego; a hazardous and nerve-racking sport in those early days. He had had several narrow escapes and one crash. He still kept an early Auster in a hangar on the air strip near Viamonte. Covered now in dust and cobwebs and probably totally un-airworthy, until a few years ago the engine had started and Beetle would taxi up and down the runway. He dreamt of flying again one day, but I fear that the nearest to flying that he will get now, are the few UFOs that he told us he had seen.

A lot of the way of life at Viamonte is still as it was in Britain in the 1920s and 30s. Conversation is an art which we have sadly lost. I spent a lot of time talking with Oliver and Len, about the wild life of Tierra del Fuego and how this is changing with the years and the encroachment of man. Len, quiet and unassuming, still walked five miles or more every day, looking at the stock, the conditions of the fences and the wild life; it was hard to believe that he was seventy-six. Oliver was the fisherman and we spent an exciting day with him fishing at the mouth of the Ewan River, a wild, remote and lovely spot below a cliff. On these days out with Oliver, he would always bring a "tucker box", as he called it, that would have done credit to Fortnum and Mason. The great grey mullet he caught that day was eaten for supper on the next.

At Viamonte, all the meals were an occasion, made possible, I suppose, by the fact that there were still Chilean servants willing to work as domestics. We sat on either side of a long table with the lady of the house presiding – usually Stephanie, Adrian Goodall's wife. When she was away, Clarita took over. Tea was like the teas I remember as a child in the 1930s, toast, scones, bread and butter, jam, cakes and buns, with tea, either China or Indian, served out of a silver teapot. Conversation ranged over all topics and flowed easily. We do not have time for teas like that any more. Nor do we live in large family units with three generations sitting down together to talk and discuss the day's work and happenings. It was nostalgically evocative for me, belonging, as it did, to a way of life that is long dead, yet which I just remember.

But Adrian Goodall, the general manager of Viamonte, now in his mid-forties, has to be a farmer of the 1970s and 1980s. Like most farmers in Britain, he, too, spends much more of his time with paperwork, forms and juggling with accounts than certainly Thomas Bridges did, or his sons, Despard, Will and Lucas. He needs now to find markets worldwide and to anticipate demands and changes in demands. A few years ago they started to shift away from sheep and wool production and move into beef, but now the emphasis is changing again and they are cutting back on the cattle at Viamonte.

Adrian had not changed much since I had first met him. Burly, red-faced and with an enormous sense of humour, we got on well then and did so again. One of my party tricks is a ludicrous sketch called "Atmospherics", which concerns the muddling up of three BBC broadcast talks, so that one merges into the other with amusing results. In my less sober moments I can do the whole sketch, taking all three parts myself, and also that of the harassed announcer. In 1963 I had recorded this sketch for Adrian on his tape recorder. He still had the recording and one day suddenly confronted me with it. The years slipped away and I pictured again Eric sitting back smiling in his quiet way, as I had recorded this bit of nonsense. For all my broadcasting background, I found it very moving that a part of me and a moment of my life was still here on tape, in an estancia in Tierra del Fuego after sixteen years.

One sequence I needed for the film was shearing. At Viamonte now there are 15,000 sheep, but one batch had already been sheared and the others would be clipped after we had gone, so we filmed at an estancia called Pirinaica about forty miles away. In these hangar-like shearing sheds, the eighteen professional members of the team were at work. It was a scene of frenzied activity. Their fee is based on piece work; the more fleeces off each day, the more money, and the quicker the team can move on to the next estancia. There were six actual shearers at work peeling off the fleeces under the rattling, buzzing shears. Everything was done on the run. There were two lads sweeping up the small clippings so that not an ounce was wasted. As every fleece came free, the wool boys scooped them up and ran to the special table where each one was skilfully folded and rolled into a bundle. With a swift rugger pass the fleeces were thrown to the pressmen in charge of the huge wooden press that packs them into compact, hessian-covered bales; an ancient, squeaking monster that was at least fifty years old. The shed was full of the sound of chattering shears, the air was pungent with the smell of newly-shorn wool and frightened sheep. The hands of the workers were shining with layers of grease from the heavy fleeces. Not a word was spoken; everyone knew their job.

This was an Argentine team, though usually they were Chileans who came over for the summer season. But there are not so many shearers moving round from estancia to estancia as there used to be; young men do not seem to want the job and it is a problem to get a team at the time you want it. These acute labour problems were not made any easier by the political situation.

This was probably the most serious threat and worry to Adrian in the running of Viamonte. With such vast areas to farm (50,000 acres now) the maintenance problems are immense. He talked about 5,000 miles of wire in the fences and posts, constantly in need of replacement. The large numbers of farm buildings and dwellings all need looking after, repairing and painting. Wood for all the fires, tons of it, needs to be cut and sawn into logs. Not many of our labour-saving farming methods would really help Viamonte. They still need shepherds on horseback, dogs, shearers, fencing teams, wood-cutters, cooks and bottle-washers; in other words, men, and good men at that, to do the work, and that is where the difficulty lies.

The final worry came from Stephanie. Since coming to live at Viamonte, she has become more and more aware of the history of the Bridges family and the aura that surrounds both Viamonte and Harberton. Over the years a great many people had come to stay, to write about the family, to make films, to take pictures. There had been inevitably, a great many spongers and cadgers who had come to gawp, take what they could and give nothing in return. But it was not only this aspect that worried Stephanie. Not only did she feel that they, as a family, were losing their privacy, but the influx of people to Viamonte and Harberton would drastically change their way of life and everything they valued. Harberton could perhaps become more of a tourist centre, but Viamonte was still, and should remain, a viable ranch. Once again Tierra del Fuego and the Bridges family are poised on the brink of a change. I could not help wondering what Annie and Abigail, Tommy's daughters, and Christina and Simon, Adrian's children, will be doing in thirty years time. Will they be content to carry on the traditions of their great-great-grandparents and still live and farm here at this "Uttermost Part of the Earth"?

11

The Darwin Range

We left Viamonte in the black dawn. I drove the pick-up loaded with all the camera gear. Just outside Rio Grande we were stopped by an armed guard, a youth wearing goggles against the dust. We were back to reality. We waved our passports and the two letters of introduction from the Argentine Naval Commission in London and said, "Ingles, old fruit." He seemed satisfied and waved us on. The plan was that we should leave the truck for Adrian to fetch later and travel by coach to Porvenir on the Magellan Straits in Chile. Luckily, Oliver had booked seats for us, for already quite a crowd had collected. Eventually the coach rumbled in and we had the job of loading the large amount of baggage into the boot, while some of it had to travel inside with us on the back seats.

At last we were off across flat, brown, arid plain to the north of Rio Grande. Oil pipelines snaked across the parched grasslands and in the distance flames flickered from the oil wells where they were burning off the waste products and gas. It took me back with a jolt to the Sahara where I had been filming a few years before.

At San Sebastian, the Argentine frontier, we were herded into a room in a large wooden hut, having first unloaded all the camera gear, film stock and our personal baggage and placed it in a huge and hideously obtrusive pile in the corner. All our fellow travellers, most of them Chilean, were made to unpack everything. Our hearts sank. It looked as if we would be stuck here for hours. Then our turn came. We showed our passports and the two magical letters from the Argentine Naval Commission. One was addressed to the Governor of Tierra del Fuego and the other to the officer commanding the forces there. The little Customs official could hardly believe his eyes. He stared up at us from under his brows and the letters were passed round for all to inspect. With a wave, he indicated that we should go back to the bus with all our gear. We did not open a single bag!

At the Chilean border it was dank, raw and drizzling. Once again we all had to get out, but mercifully the baggage stayed in the coach. The Customs official here had pebble spectacles and not much intelligence. He had a huge ledger and laboriously filled in the details from our passports, breathing heavily, his face inches from the page. The visas we had were something completely new to him. The whole procedure ground to a halt while he conferred with his officer. Each one of us had to explain in our very bad Spanish what our occupations were and there were long silences, whistles of astonishment and then finally giggles. It was a strange interlude. The only sour note was when one of the Customs officers made us queue outside in the rain rather than sit on a bench inside the hall. In the whole of our stay in Chile this was the only officious and unfriendly behaviour we experienced.

The coach rattled on, the radio now tuned to Punta Arenas with its continuous commercial barrage. We passed dust tracks, huge mobs of sheep, shepherds on horseback, rolling, dry, treeless hills. For a while we followed the shore of Useless Bay and could see Dawson Island, a dark line on the horizon. By midday we arrived at Porvenir, which very much had the feeling of a shanty town, its little houses painted in light blues, greens and reds. The coach took us down to a small dock where the ferry was waiting for us. There were large crowds hanging around and quite a number of huge lorries loaded with bales of wool. The ferry was designed like a tank landing craft and after we bought our tickets, we carried all the camera gear and our personal rucksacks on board and watched the wool lorries rolling up the ramp into the holds. Two hours late, we sailed out past a wreck and into the Magellan Straits. Dolphins began to leap and jump in the bow waves and astern as we stood and photographed their antics. We were given soup, sausages and eggs with potatoes, in what must have been the crew's quarters. The cook beamed at us through the hatch as we tried to talk to him in our poor Spanish. All the passenger cabins were full of people chatting, eating and drinking wine. The bridge of the ferry was apparently open to the public and packed so tightly with passengers that the helmsman could hardly turn the wheel. There was an amazing feeling of friendliness and informality and the atmosphere hit us with overwhelming force. There was nothing of the grim, tense feeling we had experienced in Buenos Aires and Ushuaia. Here were a people who were spontaneously happy and relaxed, with normal, friendly reactions to us. The contrast was enormous and suddenly I felt as if I had come home.

We glided into Punta Arenas and tied up at a small quay about four miles from the city. A taxi took us to the Plaza Hotel where Iain was staying. We had heard from him a couple of times by telegram while we had been with Oliver Bridges. Once, to tell us that he had arrived, the second time to ask us to get to Punta Arenas as quickly as possible, which, with our filming commitments and uncertainties about travel from the Argentine to Chile, had been difficult. We found Iain in a small, box room without any windows to the outside, surrounded by all the expedition kit bags. The hotel had been at one time a fine building, for the proportions were good, but cheap conversions and alterations had been carried out with thin partitions to add cubby-hole bathrooms and turn one large room into two or even three bedrooms. The corridors and landings were dark and drab. The drains smelt and the whole place had a seedy, run-down feeling. In the middle of this, poor Iain had waited for us in his cell. Like many people who have been alone and lonely for a while, he talked and talked and was obviously tremendously glad to see us, as we were him. He had undertaken an unenviable task and had run into problems that were now to make us alter our overall plans.

Firstly, there had not been as much help forthcoming from the Chilean Forestry Department as he had assumed and while he had met several people concerned with forestry and had travelled around a little, it had not taken up as much of his time as he had expected. But far more serious was the fact that Captain John Howard, Commander of the Third Chilean Naval Zone, who had been expecting us and had received all the details of the expedition from London, had been posted north to Santiago and his successor had not really settled into his new post. Nobody at the Naval Headquarters at Punta Arenas had heard of us and our request for help with transport to the Darwin Range. Not only was there a new commander, but he was away making arrangements for his move south. However relaxed and calm everyone seemed on the surface, it was understandable that the fact that Argentine and Chile had nearly been involved in a war occupied everyone's mind at the Naval Headquarters much more than transportation for a small British expedition to the Darwin Range.

But Iain had not been idle. He had met quite a number of friendly people who had given him advice, and introduced him to others who were in the position to help us. The most useful contact had been with Mario and Patrick Maclean, father and son, who ran a crab canning plant on Navarino Island, near Puerto Williams. If we could get ourselves and our gear to Puerto Williams, Patrick might be able to transport us in one of his crabbing boats to Yendegaia. Clearly, we were going to have to abandon our original plan of crossing the mountains from Parry Bay to Yendegaia.

The next problem was to get there. Puerto Williams was where sixteen years ago our good friends of the *Beagle* had finally dropped Eric, Peter Bruchhausen and me after our happy foray along the Beagle Channel. Then the Chilean navy had been on hand to fly us back to Punta Arenas. But times had changed, and now we had to learn how to shift for ourselves. Iain had found out that there was one flight a week by Lan Chile, the civil airline, but that it was controlled by the navy and we were too late to book for that week's flight. So we had to hang around until the following Friday. We were back to the old, frustrating, waiting game.

Punta Arenas had not really changed in sixteen years, except that its population had grown from 40,000 to 90,000, so the town now sprawled out further along the shores of the Magellan Straits and up behind the city to the hills. Mrs Nancy Stewart who had fed Eric and me so well was still there, her reputation for making splendid wedding cakes growing with the years. And the British Club was still there, but, sadly, its final closure seemed imminent. I suppose it had outlived its day. Sixteen years ago it had had a busy and thriving membership; Bert Sheriff of the English School had been an active secretary. Now the numbers of the British living in Punta Arenas had dwindled and the younger men no longer wanted this sort of club. It was almost like a film set of what a foreigner would think a British club should be. It had high, gloomy rooms with peeling paintwork and leather and wicker chairs. The glass-fronted bookcases of the library were full of beautiful and unutterably dull, leather-bound books. There was a picture of Queen Elizabeth, but one really expected it to be Victoria. Everything had a musty, slightly decaying smell. The largest room of all had three fine billiard tables and this was the room that was used most, as they were reputedly the best billiard tables in Punta Arenas. However, the club was only open from six to eight each night and a very bored Chilean steward served drinks in the little bar, glancing every few minutes at his watch to see if it was time to close. All round the bar there were pictures of the ships of the Royal Navy that had called at Punta Arenas on courtesy visits in the "good old days". HMS *Protector* was there, from the time when Eric and I had been entertained both in the club and on board. During our enforced stay in Punta Arenas this time we nearly drank the bar dry.

We also had the extremely good fortune to meet the British Vice-Consul, Mr. A. D. King, and his secretary, Mr. George Boyd, who not only saw to the booking of our flight but arranged for our gear to be taken by sea, thus saving us an enormous excess baggage bill. One day I put in a call from Punta Arenas to Widecombe-in-the-Moor which left me hollow with home-sickness for several hours, but procured us another £400, and we filled in some time profitably enough studying aerial photographs of the Darwin Range at the Instituto de Patagonia who also gave Iain a lot of help and encouragement with his seed-collecting programme. We had a mild panic when we thought that all our expedition equipment and food had not sailed to Puerto Williams, as the Chilean naval ship on to which we had loaded everything was still there. Poor Iain, who had now been hanging around for nearly a month, started talking about taking everything out of the authorities' hands and making all our own arrangements. In fact, everything was all right, for, unknown to us, the navy had transferred the gear to another ship that had already left.

It may well have been the hanging around that caused it, but our party was beginning to split into two factions. Iain and Dave had known each other for some time and had rock-climbed together in Britain. I have never been a person to try to dominate and lead in a very authoritarian way. Dave obviously felt that Iain was the leader as far as he was concerned, while Don, the quiet, easy-going person that he was, never really needed to take sides. Iain, for his part, was obviously very excited about it being his first expedition and, being an enthusiast and romantic at heart, he was full of wild dreams and plans. As I had done at the farewell dinner, I felt suddenly that I was being gently pushed out of the way. I must make it clear that there were not great, screaming rows, such as occur on many expeditions; perhaps it would have been better if there had been. But I found it an unhappy time and I could not make out if it was a conscious challenge to my leadership or just youthful, tactless, unthinking behaviour. The age gap seemed very large at times. It all came to a mild confrontation on the night when someone in a restaurant asked who the leader was.

"There is no leader," said Iain, "we are all equals, we all make decisions democratically." Which up to a point was true. It might well have been the wine talking or Iain in one of his more euphoric moods, but I felt that it would not do. As far as I was concerned, Iain could act as leader as much as he liked while in Punta Arenas, and indeed had had to in my absence. I had always looked on him as my deputy, but when it came to the mountains it was different. I was the only one who had had any expedition experience. Much as I admired Iain and Dave for their rock-climbing skills, this was a different game. Later that night, back at the hotel, I felt that I had to make my point. It might have been the wrong moment to choose. Certainly Iain was feeling ill after the meal. Sadly, speaking out seemed not to ease the situation, and, if anything, appeared to widen the rift. It was not a normal reaction for me, this laying down of the law and having to assert authority and I felt disturbed by the whole matter.

As our Lan Chile flight came in below the clouds to approach the Beagle Channel we could see for fleeting seconds below us a jumble of crevasses and side valleys leading west. All the big snow peaks had their heads in the clouds. But this was the Stoppani Glacier and we craned our necks and flattened our noses against the windows of the plane as we tried to get a better view, without much luck.

Puerto Williams, only seventy miles from Cape Horn, might have been the last village in the world but it boasted a supermarket, gymnasium, school, library, football field, cinema and radio station. Commander Gaston Droguett spoke excellent English for he had been posted to Scotland at one stage, waiting delivery of a submarine for the Chilean navy, and he was extremely helpful. On the very day we arrived he organised a helicopter to take Iain and me up to Yendegaia to make our arrangements with Mr. Cerka, the Yugoslav estancia owner I had met with Eric all those years ago.

From the air I could make out Ushuaia quite clearly away to the right, the hotel where we had stayed and the spot where the Bridges memorial stands. It was an odd feeling to know that without doubt the Argentine navy would be watching us and if we attempted to move any closer we might well be shot at. In our ear-phones, Radio Ushuaia blared out its music and propaganda.

We touched down at Yendegaia. It seemed too good to be true to be standing at our starting point, albeit only for a few minutes. Mr. Cerka was away but we arranged with his foreman for horses to carry all our food, gear and ourselves up to the start of the Stoppani Glacier, when we eventually all arrived.

Our pilot then asked if we would like a quick look at the Stoppani Glacier itself and within minutes we were flying low, first over the plain, laced with milky, glacial rivers, and then over the enormous jumble of huge crevasses. It was incredibly valuable to have this chance to clarify several of the details that had been unclear in the aerial photographs. But we knew it still left a lot of route-finding problems to be resolved when we eventually reached the glacier on foot.

Things had certainly started in an auspicious rush but now all ground to a halt again with another enforced stay. Flying back from Yendegaia we had seen the crab boat that was supposed to transport us to Yendegaia but we heard later that the skipper had broken the gear box by careless use and for this Patrick Maclean had sacked him, which did little to help us. While we waited for an alternative means of transport to suggest itself, we sorted our equipment and pitched our tents on the shore of the Beagle Channel. Away in the distance, down channel, I could see Gable Island just off Harberton, with its pointed cliffs. I knew that Tommy Goodall might be at that very moment loading sheep on to the wooden barge

The difficult looking North-East Ridge of Roncagli.

Contemplating the Dartmoor Glacier, 1979, *above. Below*, crossing its crevasses, Roncagli in the background.

he and Adrian had built, to take them from Gable to the mainland for shearing. How much simpler life would have been if we could just have come straight up the Beagle Channel from Harberton to Yendegaia! It was the end of the season at Mario and Patrick Maclean's crab canning factory. Three Spanish businessmen arrived to taste samples. Mario told us that most of their cans were exported to Marseilles. One evening the Maclean family came down to the camp-site with a great bucket full of mussels and a bottle of Scotch. We put a small sheet of corrugated iron on the fire to roast the mussels and ate them sizzling straight from the fire. The Scotch we sipped from our plastic expedition mugs. I remembered the mussel meals I had had before with Eric on the Beagle Channel and with the Alacaluf on Wellington Island, and now I would have this one to add to the memories. So very often it is the small moment such as this that sticks in the mind; the smell of smoke and the roasting mussels, the Beagle Channel glinting grey in the evening light, the quiet lapping of the water on the rocks, and beyond the grass mounds that spoke of earlier Yahgan mussel feasts along the shore.

Just above the factory a complete Yahgan skeleton had been unearthed. Had this Indian known Thomas and Lucas Bridges? How had he died? Had it been the dreadful measles plague or just old age, or a feud with a neighbouring tribe? I found a bone needle in the grave and, feeling rather guilty, took it with me. This Indian had no further use for it and for me it will always bring back the memory of the pathetic jumble of bones lying under a rock above the Beagle Channel.

One day Don and Iain made a long expedition of fifteen hours into the interior of Navarino Island to the Teeth of Navarino, the highest of which is just under 4,000 feet. They are an exciting and impressive line of rocky summits, some nine miles inland, not unlike the Chamonix Aguille, but, although they too are granite, the rock is not nearly so sound. Don and Iain managed to make the first ascent of two of these peaks on their long day.

Eventually it was the Chilean navy who found a moment to ferry us over to Yendegaia in a landing craft. We left at midnight, slipping out into the inky Beagle Channel under the Southern Cross. By first light we were at the rough stone quay of Yendegaia. The ramp was lowered, and in the early grey dawn we made our "Commando Raid" on to the land.

Estancia Yendegaia was exactly as I remembered it from my visit sixteen years before. Where we landed, a great, black cliff rose up sheer from the water. A rough track ran along the edge of the cliff to the flat beach at the head of the bay and here, literally on the beach, were the dilapidated buildings of the estancia, strung out along the shore. A skeleton of a wooden quay jutted out into the water, and hauled up above the high tide mark was a lovely old sailing boat, about thirty-six feet long. She had gone well beyond repair but my romantic nature wanted to see her afloat and sailing again. There was a feeling of being completely cut off from the outside world at Yendegaia. A boat was the only way to get here. It was as Harberton had been, before the opening of the road. The nearest town was Usuaia, but of course, that was in the Argentine, and the difficulties of crossing the border would have been enormous for the Chilean citizens.

The next day, looking like a motley cavalry made up of Don Quixote, Sancho Panza and the White Knight, we set off on horseback up the huge flat alluvial plain for the ten miles to the Stoppani Glacier. It was raining heavily most of the time and several stops were needed to re-tie on to the unwilling pack horses the slipping kit bags that contained all our precious equipment and food. I had a most painful ride as my horse was very small and the wooden stirrups were too small for my climbing boots. I had to complete the ten miles with my legs dangling down almost touching the ground. The wretched animal also took an instant dislike, quite understandably, to my trying to film from her back. Each time I tried to do this, the whirring camera unnerved her completely and she nearly bolted. The shots I took were not completely steady!

162

After five hours, we reached the glacier and pitched our Base Camp at 400 feet, at the foot of a steep, wooded gully, in a sheltered corner of the edge of the forest that rose up like a jungle, for over a thousand feet behind us. With no shortage of wood, we soon had a fire going and a brew ready for the foreman and the peon who had guided us here, before they returned to the estancia. Later that evening, as we sat by the huge fire, it seemed hard to realise that we were here at last; to me, the dream had become a reality. Eric would have enjoyed the horseback journey and the camp-site, with its feeling of being on the edge of the unknown.

But the day finally ended on a sad note for me. Iain and Dave had vanished secretly, without a word, and wandered away up the river to carry out a reconnaissance of the route. When I came out of my tent to look for them to suggest that we *all* did just that, they had already gone. I met them about half a mile up the river. The rift was apparent again. It was impossible to tell what lay three miles away up the valley, but Iain was adamant that there were no dificulties. I had been climbing long enough to know that nothing is easy until one has actually done it.

Our first problem was to move supplies in towards the mountains. Clearly the Stoppani Glacier itself was impossible. It was a grotesque maze of huge open crevasses running for many miles towards the north-west. At this point, the fast-flowing glacial river ran along the edge of the ice on the true right-hand bank of the glacier, below great mounds of lateral moraine and ice-smoothed cliffs; it was impossible to cross. Was there a way we could get along partly on the beach and partly by climbing over the smooth slabs? Certainly it looked possible, but not certain. From now on our exploratory mountaineering into this unknown area had really started.

It had rained for twenty-four hours and was still raining the next day when we set off to try to find a way beside the Stoppani Glacier that would lead eventually to the side valley we wished to follow towards the Roncagli. We were able to turn every difficulty either by following the river beach or traversing along the smooth rocks above; a tortuous route of loose boulders, moraine and polished rock, winding upwards for some three miles.

On several sections, there was a well-defined track; we knew that nobody had ever been up here before, so we guessed, based on my experiences with Eric, that it must have been made by the guanaco moving up to the high pastures.

We moved more or less as a team, but Iain was once again determined to lead and shot ahead with a "bash on regardless" attitude, as if trying to burn us off, as if mere speed would prove him a good mountaineer. It seemed so like my behaviour with Claudio sixteen years ago.

The outcome was uncertain to the end and it was with mounting excitement that we were able to turn west. Here we discovered the glacial lake we had expected to find as the result of our studies of the aerial photographs. It lay below the tumbled moraine of what we eventually called the Dartmoor Glacier. The lake itself might have caused a problem, but once again, there was a way across some steep slabs for about a quarter of a mile, just above the water, that got us to the marsh beyond. Well pleased with our first reconnaissance, we trudged through the rain back to the Base Camp.

The next day we followed the same route to the lake, carrying big loads, as we had started the exhausting business of relaying food and equipment up on to the mountains. The quarter mile of the fairly easily-angled slabs above the lake was awkward with heavy rucksacks, but we traversed along and were soon wallowing across the marsh, pushing through shoulder-high reeds. In the distance we saw a herd of guanaco and so this became Lake Guanaco. We dumped our loads and had lunch at a possible camp site below a huge moraine slope towering 300 feet above us. In all the areas where there was any vegetation there were also hundreds of burrs that clung to our clothes and worked their way up to the most unlikely places. They were an appalling nuisance and we all became pretty neurotic about them, obsessively

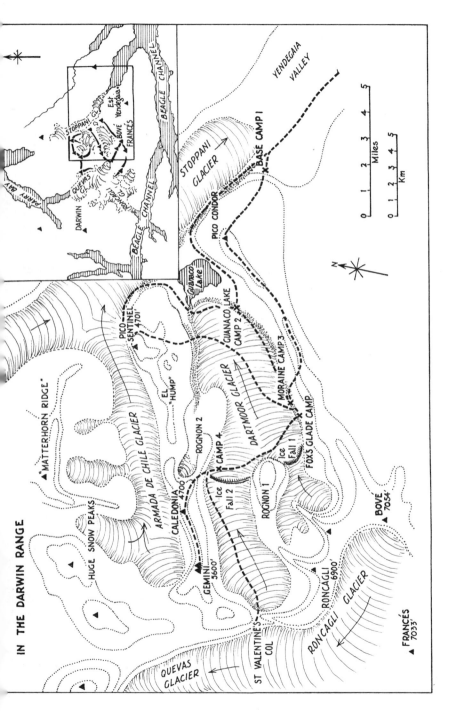

IN THE DARWIN RANGE

MATTERHORN RIDGE"

HUGE SNOW PEAKS

ARMADA DE CHILE GLACIER

CALEDONIA
4700'

GEMINI
5600'

ST VALENTINE'S COL

QUEVAS
GLACIER

ROGNON 2

EL
"HUMP"

PICO
SENTINEL
4701'

CAMP 4

Ice
Fall 2

ROGNON 1

DARTMOOR GLACIER

GUANACO LAKE
CAMP 2

MORAINE CAMP 3

Ice
Fall 1

FOX 3 GLADE CAMP

RONCAGLI
6900'

RONCAGLI GLACIER

BOVÉ
7054'

FRANCÉS
7033'

STOPPANI
GLACIER

BASE CAMP 1

YENDEGAIA
VALLEY

PICO CONDOR

Guanaco
Lake

N

Miles
0 1 2 3 4 5

Km
0 1 2 3 4 5

BEAGLE CHANNEL

STOPPANI GL.

Est
Yendegaia

BOVÉ

FRANCES

QUEVAS
GL.

DARWIN

BEAGLE CHANNEL

165

spending hours picking them off ourselves. We jokingly talked about soon getting above "the burr line"!

After lunch, we climbed steeply up to the top of the moraine, with Iain again racing ahead. From the top we looked down to the hideous jumble of moraine-covered ice of the Dartmoor Glacier. Again it was a most exciting moment, gazing, for the first time, at the glacier and the mountains we had come to explore.

The view was more or less as we had expected from the aerial photographs. To our left, the long, lateral moraine stretched for at least three miles to a point where we could probably drop down to an easier, less crevassed part of the glacier. With utter delight we saw a well-defined track running along the crest of it. We blessed the guanaco and their innate route-finding skill. In the centre, the glacier was divided by a huge rognon like the blunt bows of a ship, with an icefall on either side.

Further along, above the left-hand icefall rose a sheer and difficult-looking rock buttress for what must have been 2,500 feet, followed by a steep ice and snow crest and finally a huge, vertical, snow-plastered wall of rock, leading to the final, rounded cauliflowers of the ice bosses that made up the summits of what must have been Roncagli. A total height of 5,000 feet from the icefall to summit. If Eric had thought that the South Face of Roncagli had been difficult, I have no doubt what he would have thought about this. In Tierra del Fuego you cannot launch out on to long, technical climbs that might take several days to complete; the weather is too ferocious and too unpredictable. It looked as if most of the difficulties might come on the last 1,000 feet, where one would be completely exposed to the hurricane-force winds. It had been difficult enough to walk off the glacier at the end of the expedition with Eric. To be caught out in such a storm on this sheer face confronting us now was unthinkable. My heart sank. Iain, as enthusiastic as ever, was already planning a route to the summit, telling us the way he would go. In the Alps it might have been possible, but in the Darwin Range it was clearly not.

Further over the shoulder of Roncagli, I could see the great dome of the summit of Bové where I had stood with Eric, Claudio and Peter, sixteen years before. To the right of the rognon, the other icefall looked a little easier and certainly on the extreme right there appeared to be a way to the upper level of the glacier. Higher still to the right, there were two peaks that seemed not so difficult. Each submerged in his own thoughts, we worked our way back to the Base Camp.

Now the time had come to leave our idyllic Base, and once again we set out to carry everything we needed for nearly three weeks of exploration as far as the Lake Guanaco camp.

I needed to film this part of the march in, but I was very much aware that it was intolerable for the others to keep stopping and starting with such heavy loads. I tried to let them know the sections which I wished to film, so that they could wait for me or give me time to get ahead. The climb across the little cliff above the lake was, I felt, likely to be an impressive sequence, so I asked Iain to wait for me there before he started to climb. About a hundred yards away from the lake I filmed the three as they passed me and was left behind. I hoisted my top-heavy kitbag, lashed to a pack frame, on to my back as I saw Iain in the distance start to climb across the steep slabs without waiting. I bellowed out to him to hang on and when I tried desperately to hurry across the loose boulder field, I stumbled, got off balance and the top heavy load bowled me over. I heard a sharp crack like a breaking stick and felt a stabbing pain in my ankle and up my leg.

I had occasionally had minor twists and sprains in the mountains, but nothing quite like this. I heaved myself to my feet and, with a numbing pain in my ankle, stamped on. I was seething with rage, not only at my lack of care and clumsiness, but with the others for not waiting as I had asked. It was the only time on the expedition that I spoke out in an ill-tempered way, although there were other occasions when I would have liked to! I was aware that my ankle was fairly badly hurt, though I was able to walk without too much pain at this stage. But there was a hollow despair at the thought of my not being completely fit and well. Later, when I eventually returned to Britain, X-rays showed that, in fact, I had broken my ankle.

Our camp at Lake Guanaco was pleasant enough and there was still wood to use for a cooking fire. The stream flowed down the valley through the forest to the lake. Behind, the high, steep bank of the moraine protected us from the wind. Across the marsh with its tall, ever-moving, whispering reeds we could just see the towers and pinnacles of the séracs of the Stoppani Glacier as it flowed across the end of the valley.

I suppose this night was the peak of my depression and discontent, exaggerated and aggravated, I am sure, by tiredness and the acute pain of my ankle. Was it perhaps my lack of positive leadership that caused the problems? Iain was again full of what we should do, the way we should go and how the expedition should progress. I wondered again if I should have a talk with him and try to sort things out before they became intolerable, but as he calmed down I held back, feeling that it probably would not help. I was glad that I did.

Outwardly we were a happy group and got on well together, with a lot of laughter and fun. But had I got the balance of the party basically wrong by including two young men from the narrow, competitive in-world of top-class rock-climbing? Don was methodical and far less impetuous; temperamentally a much better expedition man. The age gap, too, seemed enormous. I was nearly thirty years older than Dave and nearly twenty years older than Iain and Don. I found myself suddenly wondering how Jack Ewer and Eric had found *my* youthful behaviour.

In spite of my brooding discontent, the next day was a happy and exciting one. We never seemed to get away early, but on this hot, sunny day we were on our way by ten o'clock. It was an extraordinary experience walking along the ridge of moraine. To our left, and about 300 feet below and across on the other side of the valley, was the dense forest, while on our right, not so far below, was the moraine and glacier; a world of rock, ice and snow. The contrast was astonishing. We were poised between the two. We followed the guanaco track for over three miles. Quite often we could see their foot marks and droppings. With such a track to follow, it was hard to believe that we were really the first people along here. We dropped steeply down to the loose moraine sliding, slipping and scree running. Once on the glacier it was easy going; it was almost free of crevasses and, as there was no snow, those that were there were easily visible.

Below the towering 1,000-foot East Face of the rognon, the crevasses became more complicated and numerous. We put on our crampons and zig-zagged our way up towards the icefall at the right of the rock face. We were soon at grips with it. For Dave it was the first time that he had ever worn crampons and had been on ice.

We first moved into the jumble of rotten ice towers and blocks, of the main part of the icefall. The temperature was well above freezing; we were, after all, still only at about 2,000 feet. It was like climbing on soft, soggy meringue. All my instincts told me that it was foolhardy to be climbing in this dangerous place. We climbed easily for about 200 feet or so and, as the route became more difficult, we heard the sound of an avalanche of ice blocks quite close to where we were. We had no difficulty in making the decision that this was not a safe way. We cramponed and front-pointed our way down as if every step was booby-trapped. Later we often watched ice avalanches sweep the route where we had been.

After this treacherous interlude we moved further right and climbed easily up through the big, open crevasses, over frail snow bridges, and saw that there was a possible way, as I had suspected, to the higher part of the Dartmoor Glacier. We tried an alternative route back to the moraine to see if there were any advantages but there were none.

Once back on the moraine, Iain and Dave dropped down to the far side of the forest to see if there was a guanaco track on the bottom of the valley. Eventually we all met up again at the camp. It had been a good day, spoilt for me only by my extremely painful and swollen ankle. At last we were beginning to work and move together as a team.

We were now developing a pattern of pushing ahead for a reconnaissance and then consolidating the position by relaying the food and equipment the next day. The highway along the moraine made this easier than usual, but the loads were heavy and awkward. We each went our own pace here, which was probably a good thing as I was moving very slowly with my wretched ankle. Whenever I was with the others I filmed our progress, but for a lot of the two and a half hours I was alone and did the usual retreating inside myself to mull over thoughts about the film or the rest of the expedition.

We found an ideal camp-site in a small glade in a hollow on the top of the moraine and after dumping the loads, set off back along the guanaco track to the old camp. A foul brew of mint cake, sweets and jam, as the tea and coffee had been carried to the new moraine camp, did not do much for us! Then it was off again, back along the moraine with full loads.

A new type of pain started in my ankle in a different place and I limped along in the heavy rain in the depths of black depression. The rain had released a new lot of scents; wet grass, leaf mould from the forest far below and on one section I had the distinct smell of guanaco, a musty, acrid, foxy odour. The others were into the new camp ahead of me and I could smell the wood smoke of the fire drifting down the moraine in the drizzle.

We now had the misery of putting up the tents and cooking and eating supper in the heavy torrential rain, with the water running down our necks. We all crawled into the soaking, steaming tents early that night to go through the struggle of getting out of the wet clothes without covering everything else in water. It was a question of slow, methodical organisation, once inside. I was glad that I shared a tent with Don, who was a great organiser, checking meticulously through his carefully-packed belongings each night. We both had a system of putting things away, each going through a set routine when we went to bed.

Outside, for most of the night, the wind roared through

the trees in sudden thundering gusts, with a sound almost like an avalanche. As the violent eddies shook the trees above our tents, the rain drops rattled on the fly sheet like shot.

The storm died out in the early hours of the morning and we decided to double load all the gear across the glacier, below the huge, towering rognon and the icefall, and find a camp-site. My ankle was by now enormously swollen and I had to struggle, often for as long as twenty minutes, to get the boot on. With heavy loads, we twisted and wove our way through the crevasses. The route we had attempted through the icefall looked even more treacherous than at first; perhaps it was our intimate knowledge of it, that made it seem so.

We found a great sheltered bowl in the glacier just beyond the icefall and felt this would be a good camp site, out of the track of previous ice avalanches, so we dumped our loads and trudged back to the moraine camp. Flat ground and up hill were not too bad for my ankle, but down hill, especially on loose rocks and boulders, it was extremely painful. Iain suggested that I should not climb up the moraine to the camp site, only to have to clamber down again 200 feet on shifting, slipping rocks with a heavy load; the three of them would share my load until they reached where I was waiting. This was the other Iain, thoughtful, kind and concerned. I gratefully accepted.

It started to blow, driving stinging sleet as we carried the last load to the icefall camp, but eased as we put the tents up and dug ourselves in. Away from the forest, we now had to rely on our paraffin pressure stoves for cooking. Finding paraffin had been a problem and the splendid Chilean navy had given us two gallons of helicopter fuel for the stove. It roared into life and burned with a hot, clear flame with that evocative smell and noise. Luckily, there was water in a crevasse to be collected for our cooking, and we soon had a meal brewing.

There were several big slides of ice above us in the icefall and we tensed each time and listened until the sound had died away, and then relaxed as the avalanche did not appear to come anywhere near us. I crawled into my sleeping bag early to rest my ankle, while the others went glissading and practising cutting steps in ice. I felt content and more at ease. We were established on the glacier, poised for the next stage.

We had seen on the aerial photographs and on the very sketchy maps of the area, that there was a col at the head of the Dartmoor Glacier that led down, we hoped, to the great glaciers in the interior of the Darwin Range; the Roncagli Glacier, that runs south-west to the Beagle Channel, and the Cuevas Glacier, that runs north-west to Parry Bay. It had also looked as if the West Face of Roncagli was an easier-angled snow face that might lead to the summit.

From the exploration point of view I wished to link up with these glaciers, if possible, and so complete the work that Eric and I had carried out in this region. Again, if at all possible, I also wanted to attempt to climb Roncagli by an easier route than the one we could see on the north side. At this stage, with the limited time left to us, these were our aims and ambitions.

So far the weather pattern had been unbelievably good for the Darwin Range. Almost every day started sunny and calm but with clouds, snow and strong winds arriving by mid-afternoon. On February 14th we set off on a fine morning to try to find the other way up the right-hand edge of the icefall, following the ramp I had seen from the moraine. We climbed steeply behind our camp through a series of huge open crevasses spanned by frail snow bridges to a broad, flat snow field which in turn steepened towards a corner, where it looked as if the ramp ran through the crevasses to the area above.

All went well, and by a fairly complicated route we were through the main difficulties. However, we were now faced with appalling snow conditions, that were to endanger and exhaust us for the rest of the expedition. The rain, coupled with the exceptionally dry, warm summer had made the snow very soft and granular; there were no really heavy frosts at night to freeze the snow into the hard, crisp surface that is the delight of mountaineers. We also expected there to be fewer crevasses on this high, flatter area of the glacier, but it was, instead, an incredibly complex and heavily crevassed section and, worst of all, the snow bridges were soft and on the point of collapse. Each one of us had to be belayed by others over the obvious danger zones. But it was the hidden crevasses and the soft snow bridges we could *not* see that were the real hazard. It was a back-breaking and tedious business and we all dropped into a routine. We drove the ice-axes up to the head, twisted the rope round, belayed the leader over the crevasses, pulled the ice-axe out, crossed the crevasse oneself, took up the coils, belayed the next man and so on, time and time again. We were constantly kneeling, coiling the rope, plodding on and then stopping again. There was little chance to build up an easy rhythm that is so vital in order to climb well. None of us fell completely into a crevasse, but we all had the unnerving experience several times of breaking through up to our waists, with our legs swinging in space over the blue and green, icy throat below. By lunchtime, the weather worsened to squalls and sleet, but it was vital to get to the col, as all decisions for the rest of our exploration depended on what we found there. The visibility was down to about a quarter of a mile; the wind strengthened considerably, blowing stinging sleet as we climbed on, but at last the glacier flattened, the crevasses vanished and ahead we could see the narrow col between a steep rock ridge on the left and steep ice on the right. We had made it. It was February 14th, so obviously it had to be St Valentine's Col, height about 4,000 feet.

In spite of the elation of reaching this unknown col, our disappointment was intense. Instead of the link through to the great glaciers of the interior of the Darwin Range, the far side of the col was a sheer drop of over 1,000 feet of rotten ice and loose, snow-covered rocks. There, far below us, were those glaciers that we had hoped to explore and the land-locked, horseshoe lake that Eric and I had seen. Even if we had been able to get ourselves down, the task of carrying heavy loads of food and equipment to the glacier below would have been virtually impossible, especially in the limited time that we had left. Worse still, we could also see that instead of the easier snow slopes we had expected on the west and north-west of Roncagli, once again there were sheer, difficult-looking buttresses and long, snow-plastered rock walls.

It was a long and tiring descent, wading through the deep granular snow, constantly belaying each other over the rotten snow bridges. I think our morale had been boosted by reaching the col, an exciting bit of exploratory mountaineering, but now the disappointment was there and also the problem of what to do next. Once again we pondered the possibility of the great rock buttress, curved ice crest and steep snow-covered rock wall of Roncagli. Reluctantly we all agreed that it was not for us – if anyone. Dave and Iain found out how loose and rotten the rock was, one day, when they did some rock climbing on the rognon.

We had several festering days in the camp, either because the weather was poor or because we needed a rest day. As always we·became bored by the inactivity, and the other three spent quite a bit of time abseiling into crevasses, practising ice-climbing techniques from the glacier and glissading on the atrocious snow, while I rested my ankle. We were beginning to bind more into a team and the competitiveness and aggression were not so apparent. It is strange how a group of males, especially in such situations as an expedition, reverts to crude and often puerile humour. There were moments that were genuinely funny by any standards, but most of the humour was of the "bum and tits" variety, with farts and belches bringing the house down. Catchphrases also seem to emerge on expeditions, and it was strange, too, how we would all talk in different accents. Devon, of course, but North Country of the music hall type and Scots were popular. It was almost as if we were retreating behind a disguise of voices to protect the privacy of our own inward-looking worlds, especially perhaps, myself. Iain and Dave talked together more than Don and I did and enjoyed playing cards. Hysterical, wild laughter would come floating out of their tent till late at night. I felt

Don would have enjoyed the games too and indeed on several nights they made up a threesome in our tent.

We all developed little quirks. Iain would wander about humming tunelessly and groaning gently to himself. Dave would suddenly croon a single line from some pop song – never any more; the rest would be going on in his head, I suspected. Don was prone to sudden fits of eccentricity. Normally a quiet, placid man, he would go leaping off barefoot across the snow to fetch water.

Our icefall camp was very well protected from prevailing winds, but we all felt an apprehension about avalanches and could never get used to the sound of collapsing séracs. Each time they fell we would hold our breath and wait till the sound rumbled and boomed away to silence. Our observations and common sense told us that we were safe, but the emotions and the instinct pumped the adrenalin round inside us each time. The cold, of course, struck up through our foam mats, air mattresses and sleeping bags, and the glacier inched on its way with sudden cracks and judders, squeaks and groans, like a huge living monster.

We were incredibly lucky with the weather. Only on one night did we experience anything like the storms I had seen with Eric, with hurricane force winds driving rattling sleet and snow. We had seen, away to the north-west of our camp, two high snow peaks and we now decided to carry out a reconnaissance towards them and explore that area.

To do this, Iain and I set out from our icefall camp to climb steep and granulated snow through yet another complex area of séracs and crevasses. Eventually we reached a plateau of ice with outcrops of rocks, still surprisingly very crevassed in an incredibly haphazard fashion. Quite close, to the north-west, we could see a small peak, which we had noticed from our moraine camp, and we decided to make a first ascent of this, as it would be a good vantage point.

The bad weather always seemed to hit us at about 4,000 feet and in strengthening wind, that whipped stinging sleet at our faces, we climbed along the steep snow slope. The wind seemed to try to pluck us from our holds and in the more violent flurries there was nothing to do but drive the ice-axe into the soft snow and hang on. Eventually we reached a summit plateau with outcrops of rock. After lunch in a sheltered corner, we climbed the final ice slope and small rock tower to the summit. Iain and I had made a first ascent together. From this mountain, nearly 5,000 feet high, which we named Cerro Caledonia after our sponsors, we had the misery of realising that a way across to the two big snow peaks that we were interested in was impossible. Cerro Caledonia was part of a long ridge with three major peaks on it, and the north side of this ridge dropped sheer for over 1,500 feet to another glacier that ran parallel to our Dartmoor Glacier. This new glacier, which we named Armada de Chile, joined the Stoppani with the Roncagli and the Cuevas Glaciers. Our two high snow peaks lay to the north of it. Once again our way was barred, but this is what exploratory mountaineering in an unknown area is all about, and the tantalising views below us towards the west were tremendously exciting. We were disappointed, obviously, but at least we were fitting the pieces of the jig-saw together.

The most westerly of the three peaks of the long ridge was a fine-looking snow and rock mountain above St. Valentine's Col. It was clear that this should be our next objective. The easiest route up this mountain, probably, was to follow the Dartmoor Glacier almost to St. Valentine's Col and then strike north up a long, snow ridge that had one section of séracs and crevasses. Iain felt that, because the crevasses on the glacier below were in such a dangerous condition, the approach to the peak could be made along the ridge from Cerro Caledonia. From our vantage point, I thought the final steep rock section might prove difficult.

The wind was now ferociously strong and the snow granules whirled madly about, as we descended. If we wore our snow goggles they became steamed up and covered with snow; when we took them off we were blinded with the sleet. On our way down, we experienced that same wild humour which comes with near disaster, as when Peter Bruchhausen skidded off on the ice slope sixteen years before.

Climbing the icefall of the Dartmoor Glacier.

Left: the steep and rotten slopes of Pico Gemini. *Below:* looking back over Guanaco Lake to the Stoppani Glacier, showing the slabs we had to traverse.

At one stage, I got a crampon caught on the straps of the other and fell flat on my face in the deep, wet snow. I was so firmly entangled I could not get up and Iain had to come and release me, weeping with laughter. The second incident occurred while I was filming. I had asked Iain to go ahead through a very complex section of crevasses and snow bridges, but he missed the route and broke through the surface of the snow, nearly to disappear into the depths, and once again we both howled with laughter. It had been a good, exciting day both for exploratory mountaineering and companionship. Poor Don had flogged all the way back down to base Camp to fetch some more rations. This was typical of Don. It was an unenviable and dull job, but on it could have hinged further successes. We hardly had the heart to tell him what the climbing to the vantage point of Cerro Caledonia had told us.

We could not move over St Valentine's to the interior. We could not now go north to attempt the two big snow peaks. We had not enough time to try to find a way round the Stoppani Glacier and to relay loads and try to get on to the Armada de Chile Glacier, either to climb the snow peaks from there or to reach the interior this way. We had committed ourselves to this valley and now had to make the best use of the time left to us to carry out a thorough exploration of the area. The peak to the north of St Valentine's Col was to be the next objective.

I was now faced with one of those appalling decisions with which no one could help. My twisted ankle had been giving me increasingly considerable pain. Getting my boot on each day was agony and took a long time. I was clumsy and awkward going down hill; I virtually had to hop on one leg, using my ice-axe as a sort of crutch. But, in spite of this, I had managed well enough. However, I realised that I could now be a hindrance and even a hazard to the rest of the party when they set out to climb the peak above St. Valentine's Col. It was clearly going to be a long mountain day and any delay could have been disastrous.

My painful descent from Cerro Caledonia more or less

made up my mind for me, but in the days that followed I changed it a hundred times. I would stamp outside the tent testing the ankle and for a while it would seem all right, but then an awkward move would make something click inside and there would be a stabbing pain to convince me once again that it would be a foolhardy mistake to go.

It had been a night of high winds and sleet, but by dawn it was easing and I cooked breakfast at seven thirty to help get the three on their way as quickly as possible. As they prepared to set off, the weather improved tremendously and by nine-thirty they departed. I was still dithering and wanting desperately to go with them, but I had made my decision and it was too late to change now.

I filmed them as they climbed the steep snow slopes above the camp, three little dots zig-zagging their way up through the crevasses, following the track that Iain and I had made on our ascent of Cerro Caledonia. I watched till they disappeared and then went back to camp to wash up and tidy the litter away. At this stage it was still a blue, warm, sunny day at our icefall camp but by twelve o'clock high cirrus clouds were beginning to edge in and the weather looked as if it were deteriorating. I decided to wander down the glacier below the rognon and look at the left-hand icefall. Using the telephoto lens on my camera I was able to see the three of them on the rounded snow slopes, below the steep section that led to the rock prow which had looked so difficult from Cerro Caledonia. I saw them sit down, I presume for lunch as it was one fifteen, so I also had mine of cheese and biscuits. I still longed to be with them and, of course, my ankle seemed to be much better as I worked my way down below the icefall to get a good view of a possible route up it.

As I trudged back to the camp at three thirty, I looked in vain for the three little dots in the snow, but there was no sign of them and by now cloud was beginning to gather over the peaks and sleet was in the air. I read, brewed and dozed, wondering all the time how they were getting on. By six thirty I had prepared a huge meal, ready for when they should eventually return. As so often when one is alone, I talked to myself as I tottered about, fetching water and cooking the three-course meal. At seven o'clock, I went outside and walked a little way down the glacier to where I could see further up the snow slope. There was no sign of them. At eight thirty, I warmed the meal up again and now began to worry, wondering what to do if they did not return.

At nine o'clock, I went outside to look again and with enormous relief saw the three minute figures above the camp, coming down through the crevasses. At nine thirty they arrived. A twelve-hour day, and they had climbed the peak. I felt tremendously relieved and happy for them. The summit had had two heads, so we decided to call it Pico Gemini. Gradually, in little dribs and drabs, their story was told as they gulped their meal.

As I had seen, they had climbed easily up the route Iain and I had followed to below Cerro Caledonia. From there they followed a long snow ridge west towards the peak. With the warm sun the snow conditions had deteriorated and they were soon wallowing about in soft granules, as they climbed up the rounded lumps leading to the summit ridge. It was an exhausting climb, as they had to tunnel through to reach the ridge and when they got there, to their horror, they saw that the whole snow slope was detaching from the mountain and was in danger of avalanching.

The great rocky prow that Iain and I had seen from Cerro Caledonia was overhanging, and to avoid it they now traversed out on to the north side of the mountain, first on appalling loose snow and then loose rock. It had taken them nearly four hours to reach that point, from their lunch stop where I had last seen them. So, at just after five o'clock, with gathering storm clouds and wind, they made their final effort. Iain climbed up the crumbling rock wall, over two awkward mantle shelves, and with enormous relief and delight found himself on the summit between two icy crests. It had been a struggle to the end and the last section could have been led only by a rock climber of great ability and determination.

We now felt that we had carried out all the exploration that we could from our icefall camp and agreed that it would be more comfortable and pleasant back in the forest and our dell on the moraine. Iain and Dave both needed to start their seed-collecting programme, as autumn would soon be here and it was vital to be in the right place at the right time. By shouldering huge loads, we managed to move everything in one carry across the glacier and back on to the moraine. As I climbed up the last 200 feet of shifting rock, I paused, and saw, only thirty feet away, two foxes. Quite unperturbed, they stood and watched me and seemed to be almost waiting to see what I was going to do next. Later, in our idyllic glade where we had made camp, these two foxes often trotted by, once within ten feet of Don and Iain. They also, for some unknown reason, took an inquisitive fancy to Don's orange plastic mug and stole off with it one night! We also lost a bag of sugar. After that we took to hoisting all the food in kit bags on to branches of the trees at night.

It was a delight to be able to make huge, wood fires again and not to lie on ice at night. Our grassy meadow had deep water holes where the guanaco drank. On one side the moss- and lichen-covered rocks formed a wall for two hundred feet to the top of the moraine, and beyond lay the glacier, while on the other side the forest rose steeply, mysterious and primeval. A view of the towering, sheer face of Roncagli topped by its glistening domes of ice crystals blocked the end of the glade. This tranquil green oasis was such a contrast to the harsh world of black rock, ice and snow, of mountains and glaciers, of storms and furious winds, which was only two hundred yards away. It was a peaceful place where I could have gladly spent weeks just pottering about. However, we all had little bits of exploration we wished to carry out, to fit together the last pieces of the jig-saw. Don and Dave climbed the third mountain at the eastern end of this Cerro Caledonia ridge; a crumbling rock peak which they called Pico Sentinel, as it guarded the entrance to the Dartmoor Glacier valley. Iain climbed another rock peak via a long ridge from our first Base Camp, and descended to Fox Camp, as we called it, in the dell on the moraine. We called this mountain Pico Condor because of the large number of these birds we saw wheeling and gliding round the summit.

I had a most satisfying day when I followed the guanaco track back along the top of the moraine and then attempted to cross the river running out from the end of the Dartmoor Glacier into Lake Guanaco. I tried first near the lake, wading across the sand and shingle and then the numerous streams of the delta; the cold was agonising and soon my feet and legs were numb and mauve. One final branch of the river proved too deep and dangerous, and I retreated. Higher up, I tried to hop from boulder to boulder and again nearly made it, but one gap was too wide. Finally, I climbed back up to where the water roared out from a dirty, gaping chasm in the rotten, stone-streaked ice of the glacier. Here, huge boulders had fallen and wedged themselves into a bridge that I was able to cross to the far side.

From here I followed the other side of the plain to the lateral moraine of the Stoppani Glacier and then traversed across the steep, wooded slopes of the cliffs above it to the north-west. I wanted to satisfy myself that a route existed this way to the Armada de Chile Glacier which, as we had seen, leads through to the glaciers of the interior of the Darwin Range.

Three condors wheeled about my head, the wind whistling in their wings; I crept within thirty or forty feet of two guanaco and later saw a herd of fifteen of them, including six young. I had not climbed another peak but I had found the missing piece of the jig-saw puzzle. It was a thrilling day of solitary exploration. I had reached a point where I could see that the way ahead was possible. This was the way future expeditions would have to go, if they wished to climb the big snow peaks to the north and reach the Roncagli and Cuevas Glaciers. Was I already planning my next expedition?

It would be arrogant to say that this last expedition of ours could be compared with those of early pioneers and explorers, but for a while we had stretched out our hands towards them through the ages. I had felt the same awe and wonder for this storm-lashed, wild land which also has great beauty and tranquility. I had experienced it in all its moods; savage, harsh and uncompromising; calm, serene and forgiving. The mysterious land, with its mountains, inlets, lakes and forest had not changed since the beginning of the time that man first came here. I had grown to appreciate and understand, as my own knowledge and contact became more intimate, what the life of the Yahgan, the Ona and the Alacaluf had been like; I knew something of the deprivations, problems and hardships of Thomas and Mary Bridges and their family. I had stepped closer again to Eric Shipton and once more shared with him his love of this haunting, unpredictable land. I suddenly realised that a lot of my earlier discontent had been caused by my naïve, fruitless searching for his leadership and companionship once again. There was much of our expedition that he would have enjoyed and found worthwhile, but I have no doubt he would probably have achieved much more. But, up to a point, we had linked up with Eric and my expedition of sixteen years ago and added, however humbly, a little to man's questing knowledge of this world.

I lay beside the Beagle Channel as dawn edged up, pearl grey over the whispering water, and thought of Pauline and the boys and how I missed them, and the stories I should tell and I wondered if I would ever come again to this desolate, wild but beautiful, primeval land. I had sensed the magic and had drunk at the springs of enchantment. For me, like so many before, especially Eric Shipton, Tierra del Fuego had been my lodestone.

Who has known heights and depths shall not again
Know peace – not as the calm heart knows
Low, ivied walls, a garden close,
The old enchantment of a rose.
And though he tread the humble ways of men
He shall not speak the common tongue again. ✗

Index

Admiralty Sound, 22
Aerolinas Argentinas, 126
Alacaluf Indians, 32, 34, 87, 94;
way of life, 98; possible origin,
102; appearance, speech of,
103; structure of huts in village
on shore of Puerto Eden, 103;
gradual drop in number, 104;
canoes, 104; methods of catching staple diet of shell-fish,
105; now owners of guns, 106;
sale of mussels, etc., to passing
ships, 106, 107; collecting
firewood a problem for, 108;
author considers a "forlorn"
people, 109; wigwams, 109;
author's mixed memories of,
110; 182
Angtharkay, Sherpa with Eric
Shipton in Himalayas, 77, 114
Arctic Pyramid tent, 63; merits of,
64, 71, 81; difficulties in dis-
mantling, 82
Argentine, tense atmosphere in dis-
pute with Chile over territorial
claims in Beagle Channel, 124;
state of emergency declared,
125; Foreign Office Press
Department anxious that
author *should* film at Ushuaia,
with no restrictions on movements, 128; champagne, 132;
bad effect of conflict with

Chile on tourist trade in
Ushuaia, 134; rule established
in 1884, 141; sheep shearing
team from, 151; value to
expedition of letter from Naval
Commission of, 153; border
difficulties, 162
Argentine Embassy in London,
author makes arrangements
with to film in Tierra del
Fuego, 122
Armada de Chile, name given to
glacier reconnoitred by author
and Peters, joining Roncagli,
Stoppani and Cuevas Glaciers,
176, 177, 181

Bahia Yendegaia, 91
BBC film for Adventure series, 25,
33; film of tense river crossing,
41; author films crevasses on
glacier, 44; hazards of expedition filming, 45, 46; film and
cameras soaked, 50; ascent and
descent of Mount Bové filmed,
75; sea-lions and ice-avalanches
filmed in Beagle Channel, 89;
critical Panorama programme,
128
Beagle, voyage of under Captain
Fitzroy, 56, 137
Beagle (Chilean naval vessel), 91,
92

183